# THE KEYSTONE COOKBOOK
## A MOUNTAIN OF DELIGHTS

**Recipes from Keystone Cooks and Keystone Restaurants**
Collected and Edited by Carolyn (Kay) R. Shive and Cheryl Bennett Fenderson

Carolyn (Kay) R. Shive, Publisher

© 1987 by Carolyn (Kay) R. Shive
Solon, Iowa 52333

Library of Congress Catalog Card
Number: 87-90714
ISBN 0-961916-0-2

Printed in the United States of America
Economy Advertising Company
Iowa City, Iowa

# ACKNOWLEDGMENTS

To all contributors for sharing their recipes.
To Carol Brandt for encouraging an idea.
To Polly Pagliai and Cinde Shive for being faithful proofers.
To the staff of Keystone Resort for extending their time and assistance in this adventure.

To my husband, Jim Shive, who enjoyed Keystone to its utmost—especially, Spring Dipper.

With love. . . .

KEYSTONE RESORT HISTORY . . . . . . . ix

CONTRIBUTORS . . . . . . . . . . . . . . . . . . . . . x

APPETIZERS . . . . . . . . . . . . . . . . . . . . . 3

SOUPS AND STEWS . . . . . . . . . . . . . . . . 19

BREADS . . . . . . . . . . . . . . . . . . . . . . . . . . 39

ENTREES . . . . . . . . . . . . . . . . . . . . . . . . 51

VEGETABLES AND SIDE DISHES . . . . 91

SALADS AND SALAD DRESSINGS . . . 105

DESSERTS . . . . . . . . . . . . . . . . . . . . . . . . 119

BEVERAGES . . . . . . . . . . . . . . . . . . . . . . 145

RESTAURANTS . . . . . . . . . . . . . . . . . . . . 151

INDEX . . . . . . . . . . . . . . . . . . . . . . . . . . . 187

The high speed Skyway Gondola offers a 10-minute ride to the summit of Keystone Mountain summer and winter.

# KEYSTONE RESORT HISTORY

The name **Keystone Mountain** was derived from the 1880s railhead mining town of Old Keystone; remnants of which still stand one mile west of Keystone Village.

In the late 1960s, a group of investors chose to open Keystone Mountain, sixty-eight miles west of Denver, as a ski area. One of the investors, Bill Bergman, was from Cedar Rapids, Iowa. He worked closely with Ralston Purina and asked them for assistance with the food and beverage operation at Keystone Mountain.

Ralston became so involved in the Keystone operation that a decision had to be made to commit to total involvement or to pull out of the food and beverage operation. The decision was made in the winter of 1973-74 by Ralston Purina Company to buy Keystone Mountain and the developed properties in Keystone Village. Ralston Purina had total umbrella ownership of the resort which grew to accommodate five thousand guests in condominiums, private homes, and a full-service hotel—The Keystone Lodge.

As a result of Ralston Purina's decision, the resort grew to encompass a healthy year-round business including hundreds of meetings and conventions held in the Keystone Convention Center. Summer activities soon outnumbered winter activities at the resort. In 1978, the resort saw the need to add advanced and diversified terrain for skiiers and purchased Arapahoe Basin, five miles to the east. Keystone Resort now boasts three mountains for skiing: Keystone Mountain, Arapahoe Basin and North Peak which was added in 1984. With the addition of North Peak, Ralston Purina divested itself of certain assets within the resort to a limited partnership. The main partners now are Guaranty Trust and Prudential Life Insurance Company, and Ralston Purina is the managing partner in the ownership of Keystone Resort.

In 1985 Keystone constructed the largest single-mountain night skiing operation in the United States. The following year, the resort erected a 5.1 million dollar high-speed gondola. The Skyway Gondola provides skiers and summer visitors with a ten-minute ride to the summit of Keystone Mountain where a wide variety of skiing, summer hiking and dining experiences are available.

Keystone Resort

We hope this cookbook emparts to you the wonderful free feeling of being at Keystone and invites you to come and create your own "history" of memories.

*Kay* and *Cheryl*

# CONTRIBUTORS

We thank the following contributors to this cookbook who are Keystone visitors, condo and home owners, staff members and private businesses. The recipes found on the pages of this book are national and international in scope. They reflect the diversity of Keystone friends and supporters who live throughout the United States and abroad. We extend sincere appreciation to all those who lent their support to this endeavor.

ETHEL ABRAHAMS, Hillsboro, Kansas
KATY AHMANN, Los Altos, California
ALPENTOP, Keystone Resort

ARAPAHOE BASIN MIDWAY BARBEQUE, Keystone Resort
MRS. IVAN AUER, Naperville, Illinois
SUE BAHLE, St. Louis, Missouri
BARBEQUE AT THE SUMMIT, Keystone Resort
BARB BELL, Iowa City, Iowa
BARBARA BENNETT, Iowa City, Iowa
DOROTHY BENNETT, Iowa City, Iowa
BENTLEY'S, Keystone Resort
JANE BERGMAN, Cedar Rapids, Iowa
TERRY BIDDINGER, Littleton, Colorado
BIGHORN STEAKHOUSE, Keystone Resort
DONNA BLAIR, Saratoga, California
ELLEN BORCHERS, Pueblo, Colorado
CAROL BRANDT, Newport News, Virginia
DONNA BRAY, West Des Moines, Iowa
APRIL BRECKS, Keystone, Colorado
BERNIECE BREKKE, Littleton, Colorado
CAROL BROWN, Solon, Iowa
CHUCK BROWN, Keystone, Colorado
DAVE BROWN, Coralville, Iowa
SUSAN BURKE, Broken Arrow, Oklahoma
LOIS CAMPBELL, Ankeny, Iowa
CHARLOTTE WILSON CHADIMA, Cedar Rapids, Iowa
ANTHONY C. CHECCO, Silverthorne, Colorado
KATHLEEN CHOTT, Western Springs, Illinois
MAUREEN CHOTT, Western Springs, Illinois
BETTY CODDINGTON, Humboldt, Iowa
JOYCE COOPER, Santa Barbara, California

BARBARA CORNELSEN, Geneva, Switzerland
CURES AND CURIOSITIES, Keystone Resort
BOB CURRIE, Belleaire Bluffs, Florida
ELRA CURRIE, Belleaire Bluffs, Florida

SANDY DABNEY, Dallas, Texas
DORRIS DAVIS, Webster Groves, Missouri
HELEN B. DAVIS, Orient, Iowa
THOM DAVIS, Grand Mound, Iowa
DER FONDUE CHESSEL, Keystone Resort
MERYL O. DUN, San Anselmo, California
MYRAH DUTTON, Belleaire Bluffs, Florida

PAMELIA ECKLEY, Bellows Falls, Vermont
EDGEWATER CAFE, Keystone Resort

MARY FEEHAN, Iowa City, Iowa
CHERYL BENNETT FENDERSON, Davenport, Iowa
ANNETTE FRICKE, Monticello, Illinois
KATHERINE FROST, Englewood, Colorado

GARDEN ROOM, Keystone Resort
GREGG GOODLAND, Dillon, Colorado
GORSUCH LTD., Keystone Resort
NENA GRADEN, Akron, Ohio
GREATEST CREPE WAGON, Keystone Resort
PAT GROSSMAN, Wayzata, Minnesota

COLLEEN HALL, Colorado Springs, Colorado
MARCIA HANNISHIN, Cincinnati, Ohio
SACHA HASLER, Iowa City, Iowa
MARY LOU HATTERY, Cedar Rapids, Iowa

DEBBIE HAYNES, Merriam, Kansas
MARY SUE HILL, Keystone, Colorado
PAT HUBBARD, Keystone, Colorado
PRISCILLA C. HUBBARD, Oak Park, Illinois
BETTIE HUNCHIS, Edina, Minnesota

O. B. JACKSON, JR., M.D., Austin, Texas
CORINNE JACOBSON, Rockford, Illinois
JULIE JOHNSON, Indianapolis, Indiana
CATHERINE M. JONES, Beaver Creek, Colorado

HELENE KARSTRAND, Askim, Sweden
KEYSTONE RANCH, Keystone Resort
KEYSTONE REAL ESTATE, Keystone Resort
KEYSTONE VILLAGE SKI RENTAL, Keystone Resort
PATTI KIMPLE, Dallas, Texas

LA CIMA, Keystone Resort
ELEANOR LARRY, Keystone, Colorado
DARRELL LASCHANZKY, Littleton, Colorado
JODY LASCHANZKY, Littleton, Colorado
LAST CHANCE SALOON, Keystone Resort
LORRAINE M. LEE, Lakewood, Colorado

MIKE MAGLIOCCHETTI, Keystone, Colorado
JOANNE MANION, St. Louis, Missouri
CHARLES W. MARKHAM, M.D., Clearwater, Florida
BARBARA MARSHALL, Salina, Kansas
ANN MARTIN, Dallas, Texas
SUNNY MCNALL, Cedar Rapids, Iowa
ANNABELLE GUNTHER MEYER, Pewaukee, Wisconsin
KATHY MICKALSON, Iowa City, Iowa

JUDY MILLER, Solon, Iowa
TAMMY MOON, Keystone, Colorado

NAVIGATOR, THE, Keystone Resort

BETTY OGLESBY, Iowa City, Iowa
BARBARA N. O'HARA, Dayton, Ohio
ISABEL B. O'NEILL, Champaign, Illinois

POLLY SHIVE PAGLIAI, Iowa City, Iowa
RENE PAGLIAI, Iowa City, Iowa
THERESA PAGLIAI, West Branch, Iowa
AARON PARKHURST, M.D., Greeley, Colorado
MARLENE PARKHURST, Greeley, Colorado
NANCY PATTERSON, Keystone, Colorado
PAVILION CAFE/GASSY'S, Keystone Resort
PINEWOOD VILLAGE CHINESE RESTAURANT,
  Keystone Resort

MARCY PONCE, West Liberty, Iowa
KIRSTEN PRICE, Keystone, Colorado

BARB RATHBUN, Keystone, Colorado
EVELYN RICE, Omaha, Nebraska
DEB ROHOVIT, Iowa City, Iowa

MARJORIE C. SCHNACKE, Topeka, Kansas
SCOBLE GALLERY, Keystone Resort
CYNTHIA HUBBARD SHIVE, Iowa City, Iowa
HELEN SHIVE, Cedar Rapids, Iowa
KAY SHIVE, Solon, Iowa
MICHAEL SHIVE, Overland Park, Kansas

PHIL SHIVE, Iowa City, Iowa
JANET SIMON, Mount Hood, Oregon
SKI TIP LODGE, Keystone Resort
SNOWFLAKE SHOP, Keystone Resort
SOUP'S ON, Keystone Resort
NANCY SPENCER, Lakewood, Colorado
WILMA SYKES, Englewood, Colorado

ANNA VIECELLI, Dillon, Colorado

VELMA WEAVER, Tribune, Kansas
KARIN WEBER, Dallas, Texas
JACKIE WICKLUND, Anoka, Minnesota
MARIE H. WILSON, Belleaire Bluffs, Florida
NANCY WILSON, Dallas, Texas

ROBERT W. YOUNGHUSBAND, Dillon, Colorado

NANCY ZEIS, Denver, Colorado

# APPETIZERS

Continental cuisine prepared to perfection in the Garden Room of the Keystone Lodge.

# TRIPLE CHEESE APPETIZER WHEEL

1       cup flour
1/2     cup shredded natural Swiss cheese
1/2     teaspoon salt
1/3     cup plus 1 tablespoon shortening
2-3     tablespoons cold water
4       ounces cream cheese, softened
2       ounces blue cheese
1       tablespoon horseradish
1       tablespoon milk
1/4     cup sliced, stuffed green olives

*Crust:* preheat oven to 475 degrees. Stir flour, cheese and salt together. Cut in shortening thoroughly. Sprinkle water over mixture, 1 tablespoon at a time, mixing with fork until flour is moistened. Gather into a ball; divide dough in half. On lightly-floured, cloth-covered board, roll half of dough into 9-inch circle. Place on ungreased baking sheet; turn under 1/2-inch all around. Crimp edge; prick thoroughly with fork. Bake 8 to 10 minutes or until lightly browned. Roll other half of pastry into 7-inch circle; place on baking sheet. Score into 16 sections, cutting only part way through pastry. Cut around rim of each section to form scalloped edge. Cut out a 1-inch circle from center. Bake about 10 minutes or until lightly browned. Set aside to cool.

*Cheese Filling:* Beat cream cheese with blue cheese and horse-radish until fluffy. Add milk and beat again until fluffy. Fold in olives.

Just before serving, spread cheese filling evenly to edge of 9-inch circle; place scored circle on top. If desired, garnish with parsley and olives. To serve, cut into wedges. Serves 16.

*This is a delicious, elegant and gorgeous recipe given to me by Hope Birdsall, whose husband, Ted, was the first mountain manager.*

Jane Bergman
Cedar Rapids, Iowa

## SPINACH BALLS

| 2 | boxes frozen chopped spinach |
| 2 | cups of herb bread stuffing mix |
| 2 | onions, finely chopped |
| 4 | eggs, slightly beaten |
| 1/2 | cup melted butter |
| 1/2 | cup Parmesan cheese |
| 1 | tablespoon garlic salt |
| 1/2 | teaspoon thyme |
| 1/2 | tablespoon black pepper |

Cook spinach as directed on package, drain well and press water out of spinach. Place in large mixing bowl. Add all other ingredients to spinach and mix well. Shape into balls the size of a walnut. Place on cookie sheet. Bake 20 minutes at 350 degrees. Makes about 9 dozen appetizers.

*Spinach balls can be frozen before baking. These are excellent appetizers.*

Myrah Dutton
Belleaire Bluffs, Florida

## QUICKSILVER CHEESEBALL

| 2 | 8-ounce packages cream cheese, softened |
| 1 | tablespoon horseradish |
| 1 | teaspoon celery salt |
| 1/2 | teaspoon onion salt |
| 1 | cup finely chopped dried beef |
| 1 | cup parsley flakes |

Beat cream cheese until smooth, add horseradish and seasonings; blend thoroughly. Add dried beef and mix thoroughly. Cover, refrigerate until cream cheese is partially firm. Roll into ball, then roll in parsley flakes.

April Brecks
Keystone, Colorado

## MONTEREY CHEESE BAKE

1        pound Cheddar cheese, grated
1        pound Monterey Jack cheese, grated
2        4-ounce cans chopped green chilies
6-8    eggs, beaten
         paprika for garnish

Grease a 9x13-inch casserole. Mix grated cheeses. Put half of cheese in dish. Cover with the chilies. Top with remaining cheese. Pour eggs over top. Sprinkle with paprika. Bake at 350 degrees for 45 minutes. Cut into bite-sized squares. Makes 40 pieces.

Dorris Davis
Webster Groves, Missouri

## LAYERED TACO DIP

1        can refried beans
1/2    cup mayonnaise
1/2    cup sour cream
1        package taco seasoning
1        container avocado dip
1        cup chopped green onions
2        tomatoes, chopped
1        can black olives, chopped
2        cups shredded Cheddar cheese
         taco chips

Mash refried beans and spread on platter. Mix together mayonnaise, sour cream and taco seasoning and spread over bean layer. Spread avocado dip as next layer. Sprinkle onions, tomatoes and black olives over avocado dip and top with shredded cheese. Serve with taco chips.

Barbara Bennett
Iowa City, Iowa

# GREAT GUACAMOLE

| | |
|---|---|
| 4 | avocados, peeled and chopped |
| 2 | tomatoes, chopped |
| 1/4 | cup chopped onion |
| 1 | teaspoon salt |
| 1 | tablespoon mayonnaise |
| 1 | teaspoon lemon juice |
| 1/4 | teaspoon hot sauce |

Combine all ingredients in container of an electric blender; process until smooth. Chill. Makes 3 cups. Serve with chips.

Reserve 1 or 2 seeds from avocados. Place in dip (until serving) to prevent mixture from darkening.

*I created this dip recipe in 1973, and it was selected for publication in the April, 1977 issue of "Southern Living" magazine and appeared on page 118 of the book, Christmas with Southern Living, 1983. Bon Appetit!*

Nancy Wilson
Dallas, Texas

# GUACAMOLE DIP

| | |
|---|---|
| 6 | ripe avocados |
| 3 | tablespoons lemon juice |
| 1 | teaspoon chili powder |
| | drop of garlic oil |
| | pinch of onion salt |
| 1/2 | onion, finely chopped |
| 1 | tomato, finely chopped |
| 1 | jar picante style salsa |

Mash avocados. Add lemon juice, chili powder, garlic oil and onion salt. Stir well. Add finely chopped onion, tomato and salsa. Stir well. Refrigerate. Serve with taco chips.

Keystone Real Estate
Keystone Resort

## MEXICAN APPETIZER

| | |
|---|---|
| 2 | tablespoons lemon juice |
| 3 | medium ripe avocados, mashed |
| 8 | ounces sour cream |
| 1/2 | cup mayonnaise |
| 1 | package taco seasoning |
| 2 | 10-1/2-ounce cans Jalapeno bean dip |
| | chopped green onions |
| 3 | chopped tomatoes |
| 2 | 3-1/2-ounce cans ripe olives, chopped |
| | sharp Cheddar cheese, grated |

Mix lemon juice with avocado and spread on a large round serving plate. Mix sour cream, mayonnaise and taco seasoning and spread on top of avocado. Spread Jalapeno bean dip over cream mixture. Top with green onions, tomatoes, olives and cheese. Chill thoroughly. Serves 10.

Catherine M. Jones
Beaver Creek, Colorado

## STUFFED MUSHROOMS

| | |
|---|---|
| 32 | large mushrooms |
| 1/4 | teaspoon garlic powder |
| 1/4 | cup butter |
| 8 | ounces bulk pork sausage |
| 1/2 | cup seasoned dry bread crumbs |
| 2/3 | cup Parmesan cheese |
| 1/3 | cup snipped fresh parsley |
| | salt and pepper |
| 2/3 | cup melted butter |

Remove stems from mushrooms and chop stems. Reserve caps. Saute chopped stems and garlic powder in 1/4 cup butter over medium heat until stems are golden brown, about 3 minutes. Add sausage; saute, stirring occasionally until sausage is brown. Drain off fat.

Stir bread crumbs, Parmesan cheese and parsley into sausage mixture. Add salt and pepper to taste. Fill each mushroom cap with about one teaspoon of the sausage mixture. Heat oven to broil. Brush each mushroom with melted butter. Broil mushrooms until bubbly and brown, about 3 to 5 minutes.

Carol Brandt
Newport News, Virginia

## MONTEZUMA SPINACH DIP

| | |
|---|---|
| 3 | 10-ounce packages frozen chopped spinach |
| 3 | 8-ounce packages cream cheese |
| 9 | tablespoons milk |
| 6 | tablespoons butter or margarine |
| 3/8 | teaspoon ground nutmeg |
| 3 | tablespoons lemon juice |
| | dash garlic powder |
| 1 | pound cooked bacon, crumbled |

Cook spinach according to package directions, drain and squeeze. In saucepan over low heat, cook and stir the cheese, milk, butter and nutmeg until cheese is melted. Add spinach, lemon juice, garlic powder and three-quarters of the bacon. Turn into serving dish and top with the remaining bacon. Serve hot. Spread on party rye bread or crackers.

Marjorie C. Schnacke
Topeka, Kansas

## VEGETABLE DIP

| | |
|---|---|
| 1 | cup sour cream |
| 1 | cup mayonnaise |
| 1 | tablespoon dried onion flakes |
| 1 | tablespoon dried parsley |
| 1 | teaspoon dried dill weed |
| 1/2 | teaspoon curry powder |

Combine all ingredients thoroughly and serve with raw vegetables.

Dorothy Bennett
Iowa City, Iowa

## HAWAIIAN BREAD APPETIZER

2     boxes chopped frozen spinach
2     packages Knorr dry vegetable soup mix
1     cup mayonnaise
1     8-ounce carton sour cream
2     tablespoons dry onion flakes
1     5-ounce can water chestnuts, drained and chopped
1     round loaf Hawaiian bread

Thaw spinach and squeeze dry. Combine with the dry vegetable soup mix, mayonnaise, sour cream, onion flakes and water chestnuts. Refrigerate until just before serving. (May be made the day before and refrigerated.)

Hollow out bread, leaving a 3/4-inch edge. Tear cut-out bread into bite-sized pieces and store in a plastic bag until serving time.

*To serve:* Spoon dip into center of round bread and place bread pieces around loaf. As bread pieces are eaten, tear into loaf. Will serve 10 people.

*You may use rye or pumpernickel bread instead of Hawaiian if you prefer.*

Helen B. Davis
Orient, Iowa

## SOURDOUGH GOLDMINE

1     teaspoon seasoned salt
2     8-ounce packages cream cheese, softened
2     small cans chopped clams
3     green onions, chopped
2     teaspoons lemon juice
1     round loaf sourdough bread

Mix first five ingredients well. Cut top hole in bread and save the lid. Tear out soft insides and save for dipping later. Fill bread with clam mixture. Replace lid and wrap in tin foil. Bake 3 hours at 225 degrees. Serve with torn, fondue-sized pieces of bread and crust, plus or minus crackers. Serves 12.

*It's so easy! Prepare the night ahead—put in oven after lunch and you have it all ready when the hungry hoard returns from skiing or hiking.*

Joyce Cooper
Santa Barbara, California

# PAUL'S STUFFED BREAD

| 1 | 1-1/2-pound round loaf bread (rye, pumpernickel) |
|---|---|
| 1 | 8-ounce package cream cheese, softened |
| 1 | cup sour cream |
| 1 | 4-ounce can chilies, chopped |
| 1 | small jar dried beef, shredded |
| 1-1/2 | cups grated Cheddar cheese |

Cut top of bread and hollow out center. Mix remaining ingredients and fill loaf. Wrap in foil. Bake at 300 degrees for 1-1/2 hours. Reserve scooped bread to dip in hot cheese mixture. Break off bread from filled loaf as eaten.

Nancy Zeis
Denver, Colorado

# LITTLE PIZZAS

| | commercial pizza sauce |
|---|---|
| | cocktail rye bread slices |
| | seasoned pepper to taste |
| | Parmesan cheese |
| | salami slices |
| | mozarella cheese slices |

Spread a tablespoon of pizza sauce on each slice of bread. Sprinkle with seasoned pepper, Parmesan cheese, a slice of salami and a slice of mozarella cheese. Broil until cheese bubbles, about 1-1/2 minutes.

*A very quick and tasty nibble to enjoy in front of a roaring fire after a hard day on the slopes.*

Evelyn Rice
Omaha, Nebraska

## SNACK CRACKERS

| | |
|---|---|
| 1 | 12-ounce box oyster crackers |
| 1/2 | cup cooking oil |
| 1 | package Original Hidden Valley Ranch Style Dressing |
| 1 | teaspoon dill weed |

Put crackers in a large container. Thoroughly mix the other ingredients and stir with the crackers until well coated. (I usually use two wooden spoons to mix so as not to break the crackers.) If the climate is humid you can spread coated crackers on a cookie sheet to dry them out thoroughly, and then put them in an air-tight container until ready to use.

Wilma Sykes
Englewood, Colorado

## CHICKEN WINGS ORIENTAL

| | |
|---|---|
| 24 | chicken wings |
| 1 | cup sugar |
| 1 | cup water |
| 1 | cup soy sauce |
| 1/4 | cup cooking oil |
| 1/4 | cup unsweetened pineapple juice |
| 1 | teaspoon garlic powder |
| 1 | teaspoon ground ginger |

Cut off tips of chicken wings; cut wings in half. Mix remaining ingredients. Pour marinade over chicken wings in large shallow dish. Marinate at least 3 hours, turning occasionally. Bake uncovered in a large shallow dish at 350 degrees for 50 to 60 minutes.

Mary Sue Hill
Keystone, Colorado

## ARTICHOKE-HAM BITES

| 1 | 12-ounce can artichoke hearts |
| 1/2 | cup commercial Italian dressing |
| 1 | 6-ounce cooked ham, sliced thin |

Cut artichoke hearts in quarters if large or in halves if very small. Put in bowl and pour dressing over. Let marinate several hours. Heat oven to 160 degrees. Cut each ham slice into 4 strips crosswise. Wrap a strip of ham around each piece of artichoke. Fasten with toothpicks. Put on rack in shallow baking pan. Bake about 15 minutes or until very hot. Serve immediately.

Bob Currie
Belleaire Bluffs, Florida

## CAROL'S "KNOCK-'EM DEAD" ARTICHOKES

| 1 | 12-ounce can artichoke hearts |
| 1 | 4-ounce can chopped green chiles |
| 2 | cups mayonnaise |
| 1 | cup Parmesan cheese |

Combine all ingredients. Place in a small casserole and heat in a 300 degree oven for 30 minutes. Serves 6 to 8.

*Best served on melba rounds.*

Gorsuch Ltd.
Keystone Resort

## CHAFING DISH CHILI SAUSAGE APPETIZER

| | |
|---|---|
| 1/2 | cup sauerkraut |
| 1 | cup chili sauce |
| 1 | cup beer |
| 2 | teaspoons brown sugar |
| 2 | teaspoons caraway seed |
| 3 | knockwurst |
| 3 | bratwurst |
| 3 | polish sausages |
| 8 | small smoked links |

Measure sauerkraut from can with fork—do not rinse or drain. Chop coarsely and heat in sauce pan together with chili sauce, beer, brown sugar and caraway seed. Transfer to chafing dish. Cut sausages into 1/2-inch pieces. Add to sauce in chafing dish and heat through. When hot, serve with cocktail picks.

*A quick and easy after-ski dish.*

Ann Martin
Dallas, Texas

## HERRING

| | |
|---|---|
| 1 | jar Herring Snax in wine |
| 1/2 | pint sour cream |
| 1/2 | cup mayonnaise |
| 1/2 | bunch green onions, chopped |
| 2 | teaspoons celery seed |

Drain juice from herring and cut into bite-sized pieces. Combine all ingredients and refrigerate. Make in advance so flavors can meld.

Evelyn Rice
Omaha, Nebraska

## HOT CRAB 'N' CHEESE DIP

| | |
|---|---|
| 10 | ounces sharp Cheddar cheese |
| 8 | ounces American processed cheese |
| 1/4 | cup margarine |
| 2/3 | cup sauterne |
| 1 | can crab meat, shredded |

Cut the cheese into small pieces and melt with the margarine and sauterne over low heat. Stir in crab meat. Serve warm with shredded wheat crackers. Yield: 3 cups.

Carol Brown
Solon, Iowa

## CRAB MEAT LOAF

| | |
|---|---|
| 1 | 7-ounce can crab meat |
| 1 | 8-ounce package cream cheese |
| 8 | drops Tabasco sauce |
| 1 | tablespoon Worcestershire sauce |
| 1 | tablespoon lemon juice |
| 1/4 | teaspoon seasoned salt |
| 1/4 | cup slivered almonds, browned |

Reserve one-third of almonds for garnish and combine all other ingredients. Form into loaf and bake 15 minutes in a 450-degree oven. Garnish with remaining slivered almonds. Serve hot.

Eleanor Larry
Keystone, Colorado

# RUMAKI

| 10 | chicken livers, halved |
| | onion powder |
| 10 | slices bacon, cut in half |
| 10 | water chestnuts, halved |
| 1/3 | cup soy sauce |
| 1/4 | cup sherry |
| 1 | garlic clove, mashed |
| 1 | slice green gingerroot, minced |

Sprinkle chicken liver pieces with onion powder. Wrap a half-piece of bacon around a piece of chicken liver and a water chestnut. Fasten with toothpick. Continue with remaining bacon slices. Combine remaining ingredients and marinate appetizers for two hours. Drain and broil 3 to 4 minutes on each side or until bacon is crisp.

Phil Shive
Iowa City, Iowa

# SALAMI PINWHEELS

| 1 | 8 ounce package cream cheese, softened |
| 1 | pound package salami, sliced thin |
| 1 | small jar sweet gherkins |

Spread cream cheese over each salami slice and place sweet pickle in center. Roll up each slice and fasten with toothpick. After refrigerating for one hour, remove toothpicks. Slice into bite-sized pieces and serve.

*Can be made using dill pickle strips.*

Bob Currie
Belleaire Bluffs, Florida

# MOM'S MEATBALLS

| 5 | slices stale bread |
| 2 | pounds ground beef |
| 2 | eggs |
| 2 | teaspoons parsley |
| 2 | teaspoons sweet basil |
| 1 | teaspoon garlic powder |
| | salt and pepper |
| 3/4 | cup grated Romano cheese |
| 1/4 | cup vegetable oil |

Soak bread in warm water; place ground beef in a large mixing bowl. Beat eggs and add to ground beef. Add parsley, basil, garlic powder, salt, pepper and cheese. Squeeze excess water from bread and add to ground beef. Mix all ingredients thoroughly—bare hands work best for mixing. Roll into balls, 1-1/2-inches across. Fry in oil over medium heat until deep brown on each side. Serves 8...or 2 to 3 hungry Italians!

*Meatball mixture can be frozen before being cooked. Use for appetizers or, of course, for spaghetti and meatballs.*

Anthony C. Checco
Silverthorne, Colorado

**SOUPS AND STEWS**

Arapahoe Basin with open-bowl skiing above the timberline.

# CHICKEN-CHEESE SOUP

| | |
|---|---|
| 6 | chicken breast halves |
| 6 | cups water |
| 1 | small onion, chopped |
| 1 | cup chopped carrots |
| 1 | cup chopped celery |
| 1 | teaspoon salt |
| 1/4 | teaspoon pepper |
| 3 | cans cream of chicken soup |
| 1/2 | cup milk |
| 8 | ounces fine egg noodles |
| 1/2 | package frozen peas |
| | seasoned salt to taste |
| | garlic salt to taste |
| 8 | ounces sharp Cheddar cheese, grated |
| 1 | can chicken broth (optional) |

Cover the chicken breasts in Dutch oven or soup pot with 6 cups water and simmer 20 minutes. Remove breasts and strip meat. Add to broth onion, carrots, celery, salt and pepper. Simmer vegetables 1 hour or until tender. Add soup, milk, noodles, peas, seasoned salt and garlic salt. Simmer until noodles are tender, about 20 minutes. Add chicken and cheese and simmer until cheese melts. Do not boil. If you prefer to thin the soup, add chicken broth to desired consistency.

*Cheese will stick to bottom of pan if simmered too long after cheese is added. This soup freezes well.*

Colleen Hall
Colorado Springs, Colorado

## MEXICAN CHEESE SOUP

| | |
|---|---|
| 5 | medium potatoes, peeled and diced |
| | water |
| 1/2 | teaspoon salt |
| 3 | tablespoons butter |
| 1 | medium onion, chopped |
| 1 | 4-ounce can chopped green chilies |
| 1 | large tomato, peeled, seeded, chopped |
| 2-1/2 | cups milk or half and half |
| 1 | pound Monterey Jack cheese, cubed |
| | salt and pepper |
| | parsley or cilantro, chopped |

Place potatoes in saucepan and barely cover with salted water. Bring to boil, cover and reduce heat, cooking until tender. Do not drain. Mash potatoes in saucepan. Add butter and blend. Add onion, chilies, tomato and milk; then add cheese and stir over very low heat until cheese is melted. Do not boil. Season to taste with salt and pepper. Add additional milk if needed to achieve desired consistency. Serve hot garnished with parsley or cilantro. Serves 4.

Sunny McNall
Cedar Rapids, Iowa

## FISH SOUP FROM THE CUPBOARD

| | |
|---|---|
| 1 | can cream of mushroom soup |
| 1 | can condensed milk |
| 1 | can crab meat |
| 1 | can cream of shrimp soup |
| 1 | can pepper pot soup |
| | sherry |

Blend all ingredients except sherry and heat through. Do not boil. Add sherry prior to serving.

*This soup is better if you let it stand before serving.*

Jane Bergman
Cedar Rapids, Iowa

## ITALIAN ENDIVE SOUP

| | |
|---|---|
| 1 | stewing chicken |
| 4 | quarts water |
| 1 | teaspoon salt |
| 1 | stalk celery including leafy part, diced |
| 2 | carrots, diced |
| 1 | pound veal hamburger |
| 1/2 | cup Parmesan cheese |
| 3 | eggs |
| 1 | cup bread crumbs |
| 2 | pounds endive, chopped |
| 2 | tablespoons Parmesan cheese |
| | salt and pepper to taste |

Bring chicken to boil in water with salt; add celery and carrots. Turn heat to simmer and skim off fat. When chicken is tender, remove from broth and set aside to cool. Mix hamburger with 1/2 cup Parmesan cheese, 1 egg and bread crumbs, and roll into 1-inch balls. Add to broth. Cook endive as you would spinach, drain and add to broth. Debone chicken and add meat to soup. Beat 2 eggs and add to soup, stirring. Add 2 tablespoons of Parmesan cheese. Serves 16.

*This recipe has always been a favorite in our family any time of the year. I can't take credit for it...it's my mother's— Rose Magliocchetti.*

Mike Magliocchetti
Keystone, Colorado

## DUTCH ONION SOUP

| | |
|---|---|
| 1/2 | pound bacon slices cut crosswise into 1/2-inch strips |
| 2 | large onions, minced |
| 6 | potatoes, cooked, finely diced |
| 4 | large carrots, grated |
| 1-1/2 | quarts milk |
| 1/2 | teaspoon salt |
| 1/2 | teaspoon freshly ground black pepper |
| 3 | tablespoons flour |
| 3 | tablespoons milk |
| | caraway seeds |

In a large kettle, cook bacon slowly until done but limp. Add onions and saute until translucent. Add potatoes, carrots, milk and salt and pepper. Cover and simmer for 4 hours or more. Thicken slightly by mixing flour and milk into smooth paste and stirring gradually into soup. Continue stirring for 10 minutes. Serves 8.

*If you wish, sprinkle a few caraway seeds on top of each serving.*

Kay Shive
Solon, Iowa

## SWEDISH PEA SOUP

| 2 | cups Swedish yellow peas |
|---|---|
| 1 | quart water (for soaking) |
| 1 | tablespoon salt |
| 1-1/2 | quarts water |
| 1 | yellow onion |
| 8-10 | ounces salt pork |
| 1/4 | teaspoon marjoram, thyme or ginger |

Soak peas in 1 quart water and 1 tablespoon salt for 12 hours or overnight. Drain well. Pour 1-1/2 quarts of fresh water over peas in a 2-quart pot and cover. Bring soup to boil and lower heat to simmer. When soup has cooked for 1/2 hour, skim away the pea skins, if any. Peel and cut onion in thin slices and cut the salt pork into 1/4-inch cubes. Add both to pot. Simmer for 1 hour. Dilute the soup to desired thickness with water. Add 1/4 teaspoon marjoram, thyme or ginger and salt to taste.

*My family serves this soup during the long winter months of Sweden for Thursday evening suppers. They serve it with a small glass of Swedish punch (a mild liquor).*

Helene Karstrand
Askim, Sweden

## QUICK AND EASY BROCCOLI SOUP

| 2 | packages frozen chopped broccoli |
|---|---|
| 2 | cans cream of potato soup |
| 1 | can Cheddar cheese soup |
| | milk, enough to achieve desired consistency |

Combine ingredients in a medium saucepan. Stir over medium heat adding milk as needed for desired consistency. Stir until well blended and hot. Serves 4.

*Great for after skiing or for lunch! Simple but good!*

Isabel B. O'Neill
Champaign, Illinois

# POTATO VEGETABLE SOUP

| | |
|---|---|
| 3-4 | medium potatoes, peeled and diced |
| 4-5 | cups water |
| 1 | clove of garlic, crushed |
| 1 | bay leaf |
| 3 | peppercorns |
| 1/2 | teaspoon dried marjoram |
| 1/4 | teaspoon caraway seeds |
| 2 | carrots, shredded |
| 1 | stalk of leek, thinly cut |
| 1 | heart of a celery stalk, diced |
| 1 | cube vegetable bouillon (with sea salt if available) |
| 1 | medium onion, diced |
| 1 | tablespoon margarine |
| 1-1/2 | tablespoons flour |
| | fresh parsley chopped |

Cook potatoes in water with next 5 ingredients. Add shredded carrots after 20 minutes. Simmer 10 minutes and mash some of the potatoes in the pot and add leek and celery heart. Next add cube of vegetable bouillon. In small frying pan, saute onion in margarine until glossy. Add flour to onions and stir constantly until golden brown. Add this to soup mixture, stirring with a whisk to avoid lumps, cooking **no more** than 3 minutes to avoid over-cooking vegetables. Just before serving, sprinkle generously with fresh parsley.

*This German recipe is all vegetarian and is a very good diet dish.*

Cures and Curiosities
Keystone Resort

23

# GARDEN SOUP

| | |
|---|---|
| 1 | large onion |
| 1/4 | cup olive oil |
| 1-1/2 | quarts water |
| 1 | 28-ounce can tomatoes |
| 1/2 | pound green beans |
| 1 | medium zucchini, diced |
| 1 | potato, diced |
| 1 | cup diced leeks |
| 1 | cup diced celery |
| 1/4 | pound spinach or 1/2 10-ounce box frozen spinach |
| 3 | cloves garlic, minced |
| 2 | tablespoons salt |
| 2 | teaspoons mixed herbs |
| | dash pepper |
| 5 | ounces vermicelli |
| 1 | 15-ounce can white or pinto beans |
| 1/2 | pound Swiss cheese, grated |

Saute onion in oil until tender. Add water and all vegetables except canned beans. Add garlic, salt, mixed herbs and pepper. Bring to a boil, reduce heat and simmer covered 1/2 hour. Add vermicelli and beans. Cook until vermicelli is tender, about 5 minutes. Ladle into bowls and top with cheese. Serves 12.

Maureen Chott
Western Springs, Illinois


# CHRISTMAS EVE POTAGE

| | |
|---|---|
| 3 | cups sliced carrots |
| 1 | cup diced potatoes |
| 1/3 | cup sliced leeks or scallions |
| 6 | cups chicken stock |
| 1 | teaspoon salt |
| | several dashes pepper |
| 2 | tablespoons butter |
| | fresh or dried parsley to garnish |

Cook carrots, potatoes and leeks in enough stock to cover the vegetables. When vegetables are tender, puree; return to the soup pot, add seasonings and butter. Serves 4.

Lois Campbell
Ankeny, Iowa

# CREAMED ARTICHOKE SOUP

8      ounces drained artichoke hearts
1/4    teaspoon prepared mustard
3      teaspoons lemon juice
1      clove garlic, grated
       salt and pepper
3      tablespoons butter
3      tablespoons flour
2      cups hot vegetable broth
1      cup milk

Wash the artichoke hearts carefully in cool water to remove taste of brine; chop and heat them with a few drops of water until they are soft. Pass through a sieve and season this puree with mustard, lemon juice, grating of garlic and salt and pepper to taste.

Make a roux by combining butter and flour in medium saucepan. Cook a few minutes, stirring. Add vegetable broth and stir with a whisk until smooth. Cook for about 10 minutes; then stir into the puree. Thin the soup with the milk, adjust seasoning to taste and heat through. This recipe is enough for 4 very discriminating skiing gourmets.

*This soup should be served very hot. Slivers of additional cooked artichoke hearts may be added in modest quantity.*

Kay Shive
Solon, Iowa

# GRANDMA'S HOMEMADE TOMATO SOUP

2      cups canned tomatoes
1      teaspoon baking soda
4      cups whole milk
1      tablespoon butter
       pepper to taste
       celery salt or celery seed to garnish

In pan bring tomatoes to boiling; add the soda and turn heat to warm. In separate larger pan or Dutch oven add milk and butter and heat to hot, but not boiling. Add the tomatoes and continue to cook just until heated through. Add pepper to taste. Pour into serving bowls and pass the celery salt and crackers. Serves 6.

*Be sure to add the soda to the tomatoes or they will curdle the milk. You may add celery and/or onions to this recipe if you prefer, but we like it as is. This is a traditional dish served with other soups on Christmas Eve.*

Jody Laschanzky
Littleton, Colorado

# BEAN SOUP WITH APPLES

| 1 | pound green beans |
| 1/4 | pound potatoes, peeled and diced |
| 2 | quarts beef stock |
| 1 | bunch summer savory |
| 1 | pound tart apples, peeled, cored, and sliced |
| 1/4 | pound slab bacon, diced |
| 1 | onion, finely chopped |
| 4 | teaspoons flour |
| 2 | teaspoons vinegar |
| | salt |
| | sugar |

Remove the strings from the beans, if necessary, then cut them diagonally into small pieces. Put the beans in a saucepan with the potatoes and stock. Bring to a boil, then simmer for 45 minutes. Add the summer savory and continue simmering for 5 minutes. Stir in the apples and simmer for 10 more minutes. Meanwhile, fry the bacon and onion together in a skillet until they are lightly browned. Sprinkle the flour over the bacon and stir in well. Cook for 1 minute, then gradually stir in about 1/2 cup of the stock from the saucepan. Stir the bacon mixture into the soup in the saucepan. Add the vinegar with salt and sugar to taste. Simmer, stirring, until the soup has thickened, then serve. Serves 6 to 8.

Sacha Hasler                     Iowa City, Iowa


# OREGON BEAN SOUP

| 1-1/2 | cups dry Northern beans (soaked overnight) |
| 2 | quarts water |
| 1 | smoked ham hock |
| 1 | medium potato, cut up |
| 1 | medium onion, chopped |
| 1/2 | cup chopped celery |
| 1 | garlic clove, minced |
| | salt and pepper to taste |
| | fresh parsley for garnish |

Drain beans that have been soaked overnight in water. Add 2 quarts fresh water and ham hock to kettle. Bring to boil, lower heat and simmer 2 hours. Add vegetables and simmer one more hour. Remove and cut up ham hock. Place ham plus one cup beans from soup into blender and process until smooth. Stir blended mixture into soup. Season with salt and pepper to taste. Garnish each serving with sprig of fresh parsley. Serves 8.

Janet Simon                     Mount Hood, Oregon

## WORLD'S GREATEST VEGETABLE SOUP

| 12 | cups water |
|----|-----------|
| 2 | 16-ounce cans V-8 juice |
| 4 | large carrots, in 1-inch slices |
| 1/2 | medium green pepper, chopped |
| 1 | small onion, chopped |
| 1 | 4-inch diameter head of cabbage, chopped |
| 2 | 10-inch celery stalks with leaves, chopped |
| 1 | teaspoon salt |
| 1 | teaspoon parsley |
| 1 | package Knorr vegetable soup mix |
| 1 | package Lipton onion soup mix |
| 2 | beef bouillon cubes |
| 4 | ounces raw noodles |

In large covered pot, bring water and V-8 juice to boil. Add carrots, green pepper, onion, cabbage and celery and reduce heat to simmer. Stir frequently with wooden spoon. After 2 hours add remaining ingredients except the noodles. Simmer 30 minutes. Add noodles and cook 10 minutes longer.

Marcia Hannishin
Cincinnati, Ohio

## EASY BOOKBINDER'S SEAFOOD BISQUE

| 1 | can tomato soup |
|----|-----------|
| 1 | can green pea soup |
| 1 | can either lobster meat or shrimp |
| 1/2 | pint cream |
| 2 | ounces sherry or vermouth |

Combine all ingredients and heat to simmer. Serve with extra sherry.

Dorris Davis
Webster Groves, Missouri

## PUMPKIN BISQUE

| 2 | cups pumpkin puree, fresh or canned |
| 4 | tablespoons butter |
| 2 | carrots, chopped |
| 2 | onions, chopped |
| 2 | stalks celery, chopped |
| 1/2 | teaspoon nutmeg |
| 1/2 | teaspoon white pepper |
| | salt to taste |
| 1 | quart chicken broth |
| 1 | cup heavy cream |
| | dash cayenne pepper to taste |
| 2 | tablespoons parsley, chopped |
| | sherry to taste |

If using fresh pumpkin, cut in half, remove seeds and bake 1 hour or until soft. Scrape pulp and set aside. Melt butter in a 2-quart saucepan and saute vegetables briefly. Add seasonings and chicken broth and cook until vegetables are very tender, about 20 to 30 minutes. Put in food processor along with pumpkin and process until smooth, puree in blender, or push through a sieve. Return to pot, add cream and cayenne. Taste and adjust seasonings. May be prepared ahead to this point. When ready to serve, heat just to boiling point. Sprinkle parsley and sherry on each serving. Serves 6 to 8.

*Heated plates help to keep the soup hot. If you want to be very fancy, you can hollow out another pumpkin, bake until tender and use it as a tureen to serve from the table.*

Meryl O. Dun
San Anselmo, California

28

## SHRIMP BISQUE

2    cups chicken broth
1    large can evaporated milk
1    can pepper pot soup
1    teaspoon curry powder
1    can shrimp or crab meat

Combine ingredients and heat. Do not allow to boil.

*Extremely rich and delicious.*

Jane Bergman
Cedar Rapids, Iowa

## TAKE YOUR CHOICE CHOWDER

1/4    cup sliced celery
2    tablespoons chopped onion
1    tablespoon butter
1    can cream of potato soup
1/2    soup can of milk
1/2    soup can of water
1    can clams, crab or shrimp, drained
1    can tuna or any flaked fish, drained

Saute celery and onion in butter. Add remaining ingredients and heat until hot.

Jane Bergman
Cedar Rapids, Iowa

# CHEERY CHOWDER

| | |
|---|---|
| 1 | garlic clove, peeled and minced |
| 1 | onion, peeled and finely chopped |
| 1 | cup mushrooms, sliced |
| 3 | tablespoons unsalted butter |
| 3 | tablespoons flour |
| 2 | cups half and half |
| 1 | 13-3/4-ounce can chicken broth |
| 1 | pound extra sharp Cheddar cheese, grated |
| 6 | ounces cooked smoked ham, julienned |
| 1 | tablespoon Worcestershire sauce |
| 1 | cup broccoli flowerets, cooked until tender |
| 1 | cup carrots, sliced and cooked until tender |
| 3/4 | cup cooked corn kernels |
| | salt and pepper to taste |

In a large saucepan, saute garlic, onion and mushrooms in butter over low heat, stirring occasionally for 10 minutes or until onions are softened. Add flour and stir over low heat for 1 minute. Slowly stir in half and half and chicken broth. Cook, still stirring, until slightly thickened and smooth. Simmer 2 minutes. Gradually add grated Cheddar cheese, blending until cheese is melted. Do not allow chowder to boil at any time. Add ham, Worcestershire sauce, broccoli, carrots, corn and salt and pepper to taste. Heat chowder over moderately low heat until hot. Serves 6.

*This is a hearty all-in-one meal and takes only 15 minutes to prepare. Serve with crackers and white wine.*

Marcy Ponce
West Liberty, Iowa

30

## ALFIE PACKER STEW

| | |
|---|---|
| 1 | medium onion, sliced thin |
| 2 | tablespoons salad oil |
| 2 | pounds ground chuck |
| 2 | 1-pound cans tomatoes |
| 3 | minced garlic cloves |
| 5 | tablespoons chili powder |
| 2 | teaspoons sugar |
| 1/4 | cup cold water |
| 4 | stalks celery, sliced diagonally |
| 1 | 16-ounce can kidney beans, drained |
| 1 | 16-ounce can green beans, drained |
| 6 | fresh mushrooms, sliced |
| 1/4 | cup flour |
| 1/4 | cup cold water |

In an electric skillet, cook onion in oil until tender. Add meat and cook, stirring, until browned. Stir in tomatoes and garlic. Next, mix chili powder, sugar and 1/4-cup cold water until smooth; add to skillet. Simmer, covered, for 1 hour. Add celery. Simmer, uncovered, for 1/2 hour. Add kidney beans, green beans and mushrooms. Heat through. In water-tight container, shake flour and water together until smooth. Add to mixture gradually, stirring, until thickened and piping hot. Serves 6.

Nancy Patterson
Keystone, Colorado

## CHILI DOG STEW

| | |
|---|---|
| 2 | medium onions, sliced |
| 1 | small clove garlic, minced |
| | butter |
| 1 | dozen hot dogs, sliced 1/2-inch thick |
| 1-1/2 | cups pitted ripe olives (chopped) |
| 2 | cans kidney beans, drained |
| 3 | cans whole hominy, drained |
| 2-1/2 | cups tomato juice |
| 1 | tablespoon chili powder |
| 3/4 | cup grated cheese |
| 1 | loaf buttered and sliced French bread |

Saute onion and garlic in butter and add hot dogs. Saute for 5 minutes and add olives, beans, hominy and tomato juice. Add chili powder. Heat until boiling and blend in cheese. Place in baking dish and cover with French bread slices. Bake for 20 minutes at 400 degrees.

*Great for kids, and great re-heated for a hot lunch!*

Polly Shive Pagliai
Iowa City, Iowa

## FLEMISH STEW

| | |
|---|---|
| 4-5 | pounds stew beef |
| 4 | tablespoons tapioca |
| 2 | medium onions, chopped |
| 2 | cans beer |
| 2 | cups beef broth |
| 1/4 | cup brown sugar |
| 1/4 | teaspoon ground cloves |
| 1 | teaspoon thyme |
| 1 | teaspoon marjoram |
| 1/4 | cup chopped fresh parsley |
| 1 | teaspoon black pepper |
| 1/4 | cup vinegar |

Combine all ingredients except vinegar in a large casserole dish with cover. It is not necessary to brown the meat. Bake covered at 275 degrees for 2 hours. Pour vinegar over stew and continue cooking for 15 minutes. Serves 10 to 12.

*This casserole's flavor is enhanced by preparing it the day before serving. Egg noodles make a nice side dish.*

Pamelia Eckley
Bellows Falls, Vermont

## EASY STEW

| | |
|---|---|
| 4 | pounds stew meat |
| 6 | potatoes, peeled and quartered |
| 3 | medium onions, peeled and quartered |
| 6 | carrots, peeled and sliced into three sections |
| 2 | green peppers, sliced and diced |
| 4 | cans cream of tomato soup (undiluted) |
| 2 | soup cans water |

Combine all in roasting pan and cook covered at 275 degrees for 4 hours.

*Great with fresh bread and a salad!*

Kay Shive
Solon, Iowa

## JIM TULLEY'S STEW

| | |
|---|---|
| 4 | pounds cooked chicken, turkey or stewing beef, in bite-sized pieces |
| 2 | medium onions, chopped or ringed |
| 2 | cups chopped celery |
| 1 | 16-ounce can tomatoes, chopped |
| 1 | 8-ounce can mushrooms, undrained |
| 2 | 8-ounce can bean sprouts, undrained |
| 1 | 5-ounce bottle Worcestershire |
| 1 | red pepper, chopped |
| 1 | green pepper, chopped |
| 1 | 10-ounce bottle ketchup |

Place poultry or meat into large pot. Combine remaining ingredients. Cover and bring to boil. Lower heat to simmer and continue cooking for a minimum of 2 hours. Serves 12.

*Can also be put into a crock-pot and cooked all day while you are on the slopes!*

Anna Viecelli
Dillon, Colorado

## SKI-SLOPE STEW

| | |
|---|---|
| 1-1/2 | pounds stew meat |
| 1 | large onion, cut into chunks |
| 2 | stalks celery, sliced |
| 3 | carrots, sliced |
| 5 | medium potatoes, quartered |
| 3 | cups tomato juice |
| 3 | tablespoons tapioca |
| 1-1/2 | tablespoons sugar |
| 1-3/4 | teaspoons salt |
| 1/4 | teaspoon pepper |

Place first 5 ingredients on a large piece of heavy-duty foil. Mix together remaining ingredients and pour over the meat. Fold foil around meat to form tightly-sealed package and place into roasting pan. Bake in a preheated 250 degree oven for 5 to 6 hours. Serves 6 to 8.

*This is a great meal—ready when you are—after a day of skiing! Serve with crunchy French bread.*

Betty Oglesby
Iowa City, Iowa

# BEEF RAGOUT

| | |
|---|---|
| 1 | pound beef, cut in 1-inch cubes |
| 1 | can consomme |
| 1 | medium onion, chopped |
| 1 | cup chopped celery |
| 1 | basil leaf |
| 2 | ounces sherry |
| 5 | medium carrots, sliced |
| 1 | mint leaf |
| | fresh parsley, snipped |
| | Parmesan cheese |

In large pot combine first 6 ingredients and simmer until the vegetables are done but not soggy. Cook carrots with the mint leaf in a separate saucepan in water to cover. Drain carrots and combine with beef mixture. Garnish with parsley and serve with Parmesan cheese.

*This is wonderful with French bread to dip.*

Jane Bergman
Cedar Rapids, Iowa

# CHILI

| | |
|---|---|
| 2 | pounds dry red or kidney beans (you may substitute canned beans, undrained) |
| 1 | teaspoon salt |
| 2 | pounds ground beef |
| 2 | large onions, sliced or chopped in large chunks |
| 2 | fresh green peppers, chopped |
| 2 | 1-pound cans tomatoes |
| 2 | 8-ounce cans tomato sauce |
| 3 | tablespoons chili powder |
| | salt to taste |
| 2 | bay leaves |
| | dash paprika |
| 1/4 | cup flour |
| 1/4 | cup cold water |

Rinse beans and put in large pan or bowl. Cover with cold water to 1 inch above beans and refrigerate overnight.

Add 1 teaspoon salt to soaking water and beans. Cover and simmer until tender, about 1 hour. Drain, saving bean liquid. Brown meat, onion and green pepper in deep pan. Add beans, tomatoes, tomato sauce, chili powder, salt, bay leaves and dash paprika. Add 1 cup of bean liquid. Cover and simmer 1-1/2 to 2 hours, adding bean liquid as sauce cooks down. When done, thicken with flour and water mixture.

Pat Hubbard
Keystone, Colorado

# MACHO CHILI

| | |
|---|---|
| 1/2 | pound bacon, sliced |
| 10 | ounces hot Italian sausage (cut into 1/2-inch cubes) |
| 1/2 | pound lean ground beef |
| 1 | large white onion, cut into large pieces |
| 1 | green pepper, cut into large pieces |
| 2 | cloves garlic, minced |
| 1 | chili pepper |
| 1 | cup red wine |
| 1/2 | cup Worcestershire sauce |
| 1 | teaspoon hot dry mustard |
| 1 | teaspoon celery seed |
| 1-1/2 | teaspoons chili powder |
| 1/2 | teaspoon salt |
| 1-1/2 | teaspoons black pepper, freshly ground |
| 6 | cups Italian tomatoes (fresh or canned) |
| 1 | 15-ounce can pinto beans |
| 1 | 15-ounce can kidney beans |
| 1 | 16-ounce can garbanzo beans |

Brown bacon in large Dutch oven or cast-iron pot. Drain, crumble and set aside. Brown sausage; drain, set aside with bacon. Fry ground beef; drain, set aside with other meats.

In the same pot, cook onion, green pepper, garlic and chili pepper over low heat 2 to 3 minutes. Stir in wine and Worcestershire sauce; simmer uncovered about 12 minutes. Stir in mustard, celery seed, chili powder, salt and pepper; simmer 12 minutes. Mash tomatoes and add to pot. Add meats to mixture. Heat to boiling; reduce heat and simmer covered 30 minutes, stirring occasionally.

Stir beans, with liquid, into chili; heat to boiling. Reduce heat; cover and simmer 1 hour, stirring occasionally. Serves 8.

*This recipe is best made a day ahead and reheated. Serve with cubed sharp Cheddar cheese and soup crackers.*

Myrah Dutton
Belleaire Bluffs, Florida

# JERSEY LILLY CHILI

| 6 | skinless pork sausages |
| 2-1/2 | cups chuck roast cut into bite-size pieces |
| 1/2 | cup chopped onion |
| 2 | teaspoons flour |
| 2-1/2 | teaspoons chili powder |
| | garlic salt to taste |
| | pepper to taste |
| 1-1/2 | teaspoons cumin seed |
| 1/4 | teaspoon sugar |
| | crushed red pepper |
| 1 | can beer |
| 1 | can green chile peppers, seeded and chopped |
| 1 | 10-1/2-ounce can tomato puree |

In a large pot, brown sausages and crumble with a fork. Add meat and onions. Cook until meat is gray. Add flour, chili powder, garlic salt, pepper, cumin seed, sugar, crushed red pepper and beer. Stir until thick. Add chopped green chile peppers and tomato puree. Check seasonings and simmer chili over low heat for 2 hours. Serves 6.

Marcia Hannishin
Cincinnati, Ohio

# BREADS

**Keystone Lake offers a variety of summer activities.**

## APPLE WALNUT BREAD

| | |
|---|---|
| 2 | cups sugar |
| 2 | eggs |
| 1-1/2 | cups vegetable oil |
| 1 | teaspoon vanilla |
| 3 | cups diced apples |
| 1 | cup chopped walnuts |
| 3 | cups flour |
| 1 | teaspoon baking soda |
| 1 | teaspoon cinnamon |

In large mixing bowl cream sugar and eggs; add vegetable oil and vanilla. Add apples and walnuts. Stir in dry ingredients last, 1 cup at a time, blending thoroughly. Batter will be thick. Pour into 4 small greased loaf pans and bake in a preheated 350 degree oven for 45 to 60 minutes.

*Each loaf can be sliced and frozen.*

Sue Bahle
St. Louis, Missouri

## BANANA NUT BREAD

| | |
|---|---|
| 3/4 | cup margarine |
| 1-1/2 | cups sugar |
| 1-1/2 | cups mashed banana |
| 2 | eggs |
| 1 | teaspoon vanilla |
| 2 | cups flour |
| 1 | teaspoon baking soda |
| 1 | teaspoon salt |
| 1 | cup buttermilk |
| 1/2 | cup chopped nuts |

Cream margarine and sugar together. Blend in bananas, eggs and vanilla. Sift flour, baking soda and salt. Add alternately with buttermilk blending just enough to combine. Fold in nuts. Pour into 9x5-inch loaf pan and bake in 350 degree oven 55 to 60 minutes or until a toothpick inserted into center comes out clean.

Mary Feehan
Iowa City, Iowa

# RHUBARB BREAD

| 1-1/2 | cups brown sugar |
| 1 | egg |
| 2/3 | cup cooking oil |
| 1 | cup buttermilk |
| 1 | teaspoon vanilla |
| 2-1/2 | cups flour |
| 1 | teaspoon salt |
| 1 | teaspoon baking soda |
| 2 | cups chopped rhubarb |
| 1/2 | cup chopped nuts |
| 1/2 | cup sugar |
| 1 | teaspoon softened butter |
| 1 | teaspoon cinnamon |

Mix first five ingredients in large bowl. Sift flour, salt and baking soda. Add to sugar mixture. Fold in rhubarb and nuts. Pour into 2 greased and floured 9x5-inch pans. Combine sugar, butter and cinnamon and spread over tops of bread. Bake 60 minutes in a 350 degree oven or until toothpick comes out clean when inserted into center of loaf.

Mary Feehan     Iowa City, Iowa

# BUTTER BRICKLE BREAD

| 1 | butter brickle cake mix (2-layer size) |
| 4 | eggs |
| 1/2 | cup cooking oil |
| 1 | cup hot tap water |
| 1 | 4-1/8-ounce package instant coconut pudding mix |
| 1/8 | teaspoon poppy seed (optional) |

Mix all ingredients in large bowl (mixture will look lumpy). Pour into two 9x5x3-inch greased and floured loaf pans. Bake 15 minutes at 350 degrees; reduce temperature to 300 degrees and continue baking 45 minutes or until wooden pick inserted in center comes out clean. Remove from pan; cool thoroughly before slicing.

Barbara Marshall     Salina, Kansas

## CORN BREAD—SUGARLESS!

| | |
|---|---|
| 1 | cup coarse yellow cornmeal |
| 1 | cup white or whole wheat flour |
| 2-3 | tablespoons powdered milk |
| 2 | teaspoons baking powder |
| 1-1/2 | teaspoons salt |
| 1 | cup milk or buttermilk |
| 1 | egg |
| 2-3 | tablespoons wheat germ |
| 2 | tablespoons vegetable oil |

Place a 9-inch iron skillet into a preheated 425 degree oven. Mix all dry ingredients thoroughly. Stir in milk, egg and wheat germ and mix well. Spread the oil over surface of skillet and pour excess oil into the batter. Stir, then quickly pour the mixture into the skillet. Bake for 20 to 25 minutes. You will have piping-hot corn bread with a wonderful brown bottom crust. May also be baked in a well-greased 8x8-inch baking pan. Be sure to add oil to the mix before putting in the pan.

*Microwave:* Reduce baking powder to 1 teaspoon, milk to 2/3 cup, and increase oil to 4 tablespoons. Line 9-inch round pan with waxed paper. Fifty percent power for 6 minutes, 100 percent power for 2 to 5 minutes. Let stand for 5 minutes.

Keystone Real Estate
Keystone Resort

## DILL BREAD

| | |
|---|---|
| 1 | package yeast |
| 1/4 | cup warm water |
| 1/2 | cup scalded milk |
| 2 | tablespoons butter or margarine |
| 2 | tablespoons sugar |
| 1 | teaspoon salt |
| 2 | teaspoons dill weed |
| 1 | tablespoon minced onion |
| 1 | egg, beaten |
| 2 | cups flour |

Dissolve yeast in warm water and set aside to proof. Scald milk and add butter, sugar, salt, dill weed and onion. Cool until lukewarm. Add yeast mixture and egg. Add flour enough for "soft dough" that you can handle. Knead dough until it feels elastic. Shape into ball in bowl and cover with cloth. Let rise until double in bulk, about 1 hour. Place loaf into a 9x5x2-3/4-inch greased pan. Bake in a preheated 350 degree oven for 30 to 40 minutes or until bread sounds hollow when tapped.

Dorothy Bennett
Iowa City, Iowa

# RYE BREAD

| 2 | cups very hot water |
| 1/4 | cup brown sugar |
| 1/4 | cup light molasses |
| 2 | packages dry yeast |
| 2 | cups rye flour |
| 2 | teaspoons salt |
| 3 | tablespoons vegetable oil |
| 1/4 | cup caraway seeds |
| 4-1/2 | cups all-purpose flour |
| | margarine |
| 1/4 | cup caraway seed |

Place water, sugar and molasses in mixing bowl and beat at low speed until sugar is dissolved. Cool to lukewarm. Add yeast and let stand 5 to 10 minutes. Add rye flour and beat 1 minute at medium speed. Add salt, oil, caraway seeds and 1 cup all-purpose flour. Beat 4 minutes at medium speed. Bread may be mixed in mixer to this point. Mixing by hand, add as much remaining all-purpose flour as necessary to form a smooth dough. Turn out onto floured board and knead 5 minutes. Place dough into greased bowl in warm spot to rise until doubled in volume. Turn out onto lightly floured board, knead 2 minutes, divide dough in half and round each half into a ball. Shape each ball into a loaf and put into 2 greased 9x5-inch loaf pans. Let rise until doubled in volume. Bake in preheated oven at 375 degrees for 1 hour or until browned. Remove loaves from pan, turning out onto wire rack. Brush with margarine and top with remaining caraway seeds if desired. Cool.

Mary Feehan
Iowa City, Iowa

# THREE-GRAIN BREAD

1/4     cup butter or margarine
1       tablespoon salt
1/3     cup brown sugar
1/2     cup corn meal
2       cups boiling water
2       packages dry yeast
1/2     cup warm water
3/4     cup whole wheat flour
1/4     cup rye flour
1/2     cup wheat germ
4-1/2   cups all-purpose flour

Place butter, salt, brown sugar and corn meal in large mixing bowl. Add boiling water. Mix at low speed until butter is melted. Cool to lukewarm. Dissolve yeast in warm water (100 to 115 degrees). Add to lukewarm cornmeal mixture. Stir all the flours and wheat germ together to blend. Add to yeast mixture. Mix to form a soft dough and turn out onto floured surface. Knead until elastic and place dough into a greased bowl, turning to grease both sides. Cover with cloth and let rise until double in bulk. Turn out onto floured surface. Knead lightly. Divide into 3 equal portions and round each portion into a ball. Shape into 3 loaves and place into greased 9x5-inch loaf pans. Cover loaves with wet cloth and let rise until double in volume. Bake at 350 degrees for about 50 minutes or until well browned and firm. Remove from pans and cool on wire rack.

Mary Feehan
Iowa City, Iowa

43

## WHOLE WHEAT BREAD

| 3 | cups scalded milk |
| 1/3 | cup honey or molasses |
| 1 | cup shortening or margarine |
| 3 | teaspoons salt |
| 1-1/2 | cups cold water |
| 3 | tablespoons yeast (2 packages) |
| 6 | cups whole wheat flour |
| 5 | cups unbleached flour |

Scald milk, then add honey, shortening and salt. Mix together and add cold water. When the mixture is lukewarm (120 degrees Fahrenheit), add yeast, stir and let set a minute for yeast to activate. Add several cups whole wheat flour, stir. Slowly add remaining flour. Knead 5 to 10 minutes. Place dough into a greased bowl, cover and let rise for 30 minutes. Punch down and divide into 4 equal parts and shape into 9x5x3-inch loaf pans. Cover, let rise to double in size, about 50 minutes. Bake at 350 degrees for 40 to 50 minutes. Remove from pans to cool.

Ethel Abrahams
Hillsboro, Kansas

## BUTTERMILK ROLLS

| 1 | package dry yeast |
| 1/4 | cup warm water |
| 1 | tablespoon sugar |
| 1 | teaspoon salt |
| 1/4 | teaspoon baking soda |
| 3/4 | cup buttermilk, warmed |
| 2-1/2 | cups all-purpose flour |

Mix yeast, warm water, sugar and salt and let stand for 5 to 10 minutes. Add baking soda and warm buttermilk. Stir in half the flour and beat a few minutes. Add remainder of flour and mix with hands adding flour as necessary to make dough manageable. Turn out onto a floured board and knead until smooth. Put into a greased bowl and let rise until double in size, about 1 hour. Punch down and shape into rolls and let rise until light, about 1-1/2 hours. Bake in a preheated 375 degree oven about 15 minutes or until browned.

Mary Feehan
Iowa City, Iowa

## BRAN MUFFINS PLUS

1     cup boiling water
3     cups Bran Buds or Flakes cereal
2     cups buttermilk
1     cup applesauce
1/2   cup margarine
1-1/2 cups sugar
2     eggs
2-1/2 cups flour
2-1/2 teaspoons baking soda
1     teaspoon salt
1-1/2 cups grated Cheddar cheese
1     cup pecans, chopped

Pour water over bran; add buttermilk and applesauce. Let cool. In a large bowl, cream margarine and sugar. Beat in eggs and add bran mixture slowly. Fold in dry ingredients and cheese and nuts. Fill greased muffin cups two-thirds full. Bake at 350 degrees for 25 minutes. Makes 2 dozen muffins.

*These freeze very well and/or keep in the refrigerator for one week.*

Mary Lou Hattery
Cedar Rapids, Iowa

## HEALTHY BRAN MUFFINS

2     cups All Bran cereal
1     cup Bran Buds cereal
1     cup boiling water
2     cups buttermilk
2     teaspoons baking soda
1/2   cup honey
3     small eggs, beaten
1/2   cup vegetable oil
2     cups Miller's Bran
1     cup whole wheat flour
1/4   teaspoon salt, optional

Mix All Bran and Bran Buds together with boiling water and set aside. Pour buttermilk into a large mixing bowl. Stir in soda, honey, eggs, oil and cereal mixture and beat thoroughly. In another bowl combine Miller's Bran, whole wheat flour and salt. Add the flour mixture to the wet ingredients and beat. Pour into greased muffin tins and bake at 375 degrees for 20 to 25 minutes, or until a toothpick inserted in center comes out clean. Serve warm. Makes 48 small or 24 large muffins.

*Batter will keep refrigerated for a week, so you can bake as many as needed. For variety, add chopped raisins, dates or walnuts.*

Keystone Real Estate
Keystone Resort

# MIGHTY MUFFINS

1-1/2    cups All Bran cereal
1/2    cup all-purpose flour
1/2    cup whole wheat flour
2    tablespoons wheat germ
2    teaspoons baking powder
1/2    teaspoon soda
1    egg, beaten
1    cup buttermilk
1/3    cup molasses
1/4    cup margarine, melted
1/2    cup raisins
1/2    cup chopped nuts

Grease 12 muffin cups or line with paper liners. Preheat oven to 350 degrees. In a large bowl, combine bran cereal, flours, wheat germ, baking powder and soda. In separate bowl beat egg and add buttermilk, molasses and margarine. Mix well and stir into dry ingredients until they are moistened. Add raisins and nuts. Fill prepared muffin cups two-thirds full. Bake 12 to 17 minutes or until a toothpick inserted in center comes out clean. Makes 10 to 12 muffins.

*These are very good and nutritious—I guess my favorite.*

Mary Feehan
Iowa City, Iowa

# TEXAS TOAST

1-1/4    cups orange juice
2    eggs, beaten
1    tablespoon sugar
1    teaspoon salt
1    loaf unsliced bread
1    stick margarine
1    cup corn syrup

Preheat oven to 500 degrees. Mix together 1 cup orange juice, eggs, sugar and salt. Slice bread into 1-inch thick slices and then diagonally into triangles. Melt stick of margarine in jelly roll pan in oven. Dip bread slices in orange juice mixture and place on buttered tray. Bake 10 to 15 minutes. Turn once, half way through. Serve warm with syrup made by combining 1/4 cup orange juice and 1 cup corn syrup.

Jane Bergman
Cedar Rapids, Iowa

## HERB BREAD

2      sticks margarine or butter
1/2    teaspoon garlic powder
1/3    teaspoon parsley flakes
1/4    teaspoon basil
1      teaspoon dill weed
       pinch oregano (optional)
       French bread

Blend first six ingredients well and spread on fresh French bread slices. Wrap loaf in heavy foil and warm for 15 minutes in 350 degree oven.

*Can be stored in a sealed container.*

Jane Bergman
Cedar Rapids, Iowa

## PITA BREAD

8      small pita pockets
1      stick softened margarine or butter
       Parmesan cheese

Split pita pockets and spread with margarine. Sprinkle generously with Parmesan cheese and bake until browned.

*Great accompaniment to spaghetti and salad.*

Jane Bergman
Cedar Rapids, Iowa

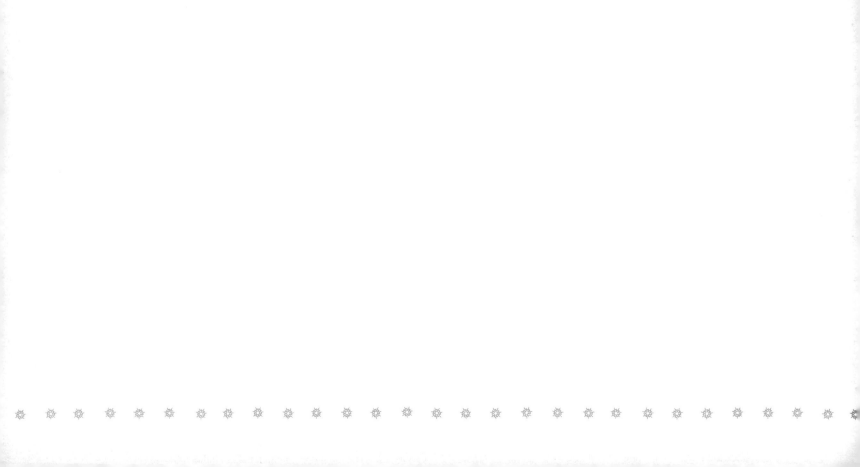

ENTREES

Resembling a giant Christmas tree, Keystone Mountain is lighted for night skiers.

# CHICKEN CREPES

1     egg
      dash salt
2/3  cup flour
2/3  cup milk
1     tablespoon butter, melted
2     cans cream of chicken soup
1     4-ounce can chopped green chilies
1/2  cup mayonnaise
3/4  teaspoon curry powder
3     whole chicken breasts, skinned and cut into bite-sized
       pieces
      garlic salt
8     ounces Monterey Jack cheese, finely grated

*Crepe:* Combine egg and salt and beat well. Gradually add flour, alternating with milk until smooth. Stir in melted butter. Refrigerate at least 1 hour. Heat small non-stick pan until hot. Pour 1/4 cup batter into pan, turning to spread around bottom and up sides slightly. Do not attempt to turn crepe until bottom is dry and crepe slides on surface. Turn and cook briefly on flip side and slide out of pan onto waxed paper. Repeat until all crepe batter used.

*Filling:* Combine soup, chilies, mayonnaise and curry powder; set aside. Liberally coat chicken with garlic salt and work through pieces with hands. Saute quickly in medium frying pan until chicken is cooked through. Add soup mixture and heat. Put filling across center of each crepe and fold sides over in thirds. Place in row in baking dish. Cover with cheese and broil just until cheese begins to brown. Makes 8 to 10 crepes.

*Crepes can be frozen individually between waxed paper either before or after being filled. Serve with fresh broccoli and a colorful fruit salad.*

Cheryl Bennett Fenderson
Davenport, Iowa

51

## MUSTARD CHICKEN

| | |
|---|---|
| 1 | chicken, cut-up and skinned |
| | flour |
| | cooking oil |
| 1 | yellow onion |
| 4 | ounces fresh mushrooms |
| 4 | tablespoons butter |
| | white wine (optional) |
| 2 | garlic cloves, crushed |
| | salt and pepper |
| | Gulden's mustard |

Dredge chicken in flour and brown with oil in heavy skillet. Place in a 9x13-inch baking dish. Saute mushrooms and onions in butter. Add a dash of white wine, garlic (or garlic powder) and salt and pepper to taste. Coat each piece of chicken liberally with mustard. Place onions and mushroom mixture on top. Bake at 375 degrees for 45 minutes. Serves 6.

*This also is very tasty grilled on your barbeque.*

Pamelia Eckley
Bellows Falls, Vermont

## ALA ARMOND—A CRUSTLESS QUICHE

| | |
|---|---|
| 7 | eggs, beaten well |
| 8 | ounces Jarlsburg cheese, shredded |
| 4 | ounces Monterey Jack cheese, shredded |
| 1 | 16-ounce bag frozen broccoli pieces |
| 2 | cups cooked chicken breast, chopped |
| 1-1/2 | cups milk |
| 3 | slices Italian bread, crust removed and torn into pieces |

Preheat oven to 350 degrees. Mix ingredients in order in a large mixing bowl. Pour into a buttered 9x13-inch dish (there may be extra—this may be baked and frozen). Bake for 1 hour or until golden brown on top. Cool 5 to 10 minutes before serving.

*You may substitute mozzarella cheese for the jack, and ham or turkey for the chicken. This is a great meal when served with a fruit salad.*

Polly Shive Pagliai
Iowa City, Iowa

## CHICKEN DIVAN

| | |
|---|---|
| 2 | 10-ounce packages frozen broccoli, chopped |
| 4 | whole chicken breasts, cooked and boned |
| 2 | cans cream of chicken soup, undiluted |
| 3/4 | cup mayonnaise |
| 1 | teaspoon lemon juice |
| 3/4 | teaspoon curry powder |
| | salt and pepper to taste |
| 1-1/2 | cups American cheese, grated |

Cook broccoli according to package directions. Drain and arrange in greased 9x13-inch baking dish. Place chicken breasts on top. Mix soup, mayonnaise, lemon juice, curry powder and salt and pepper. Pour over chicken. Sprinkle with cheese. Cover and bake at 350 degrees for 30 minutes.

Julie Johnson
Indianapolis, Indiana

## CURRIED CHICKEN AND RICE

| | |
|---|---|
| 1 | cup regular long-grain rice |
| 2/3 | cup seedless raisins |
| 1/2 | cup chopped apple |
| 1-1/2 | cups shredded or cubed cooked chicken |
| 2 | chicken-flavored bouillon cubes, crushed |
| 1/2 | onion, minced |
| 2 | teaspoons curry powder |
| 2-3/4 | cups water |

In a bowl, combine all ingredients except water. In a 2-quart saucepan, bring to a boil 2-3/4 cups water. Add rice mixture to water. Reduce heat to low and cover. Let simmer for 25 minutes until rice is tender and all liquid is absorbed. Fluff lightly before serving.

*Good for using leftover chicken or turkey!*

Helen Shive
Cedar Rapids, Iowa

## CHICKEN ROLLS

| 12 | slices bread |
| 2 | cups finely sliced cooked chicken |
| 3 | tablespoons finely chopped green onion |
| 1/2 | cup mayonnaise |
| | dash salt |
| 1/8 | teaspoon curry powder |
| 1/4 | cup butter, melted |

Trim bread slices and roll each one flat. Combine next 5 ingredients. Place in center of bread slices, roll up as you would a crepe and place in casserole dish. Before serving, preheat oven to 475 degrees. Brush rolls with melted butter and bake for 10 minutes. Serves 6.

*Can be prepared early in the day. Serve with cheese sauce. This recipe was given to me by Mary Lucas, of Denver, Colorado, whose husband was the head of the Regional Forest Service of the Western United States.*

Jane Bergman
Cedar Rapids, Iowa

## CHICKEN AND RICE CASSEROLE

| 1 | fryer chicken, cut up |
| 4 | cups Minute Rice |
| 2 | cans cream of mushroom soup |
| 2 | cans cream of chicken soup |
| | salt and pepper |
| | poultry seasoning |

Wash chicken thoroughly, removing skin and all fat. Set aside. Pour rice and soups into 9x13-inch pan and stir. Place chicken on top of mixture and season with salt, pepper and poultry seasoning. Bake, covered, in a preheated 350 degree oven for 1-1/2 hours.

Gregg Goodland
Dillon, Colorado

## CHICKEN-ARTICHOKE CASSEROLE

3      pounds chicken breasts and thighs
1      teaspoon salt
1/2   teaspoon pepper
3/4   teaspoon paprika
6      teaspoons margarine
1      1-pound can artichoke hearts, drained
1/2   pound fresh mushrooms
2      tablespoons flour
2/3   cup chicken broth
3      tablespoons sherry
1/4   teaspoon dried rosemary

Skin chicken and season with salt, pepper and paprika. Brown chicken in 4 tablespoons margarine and remove to a 9x13-inch casserole. Arrange artichoke hearts between chicken pieces. Saute mushrooms in remaining margarine until just tender. Sprinkle flour over mushrooms and stir in broth, sherry and rosemary. Cook until slightly thickened. Pour over chicken and artichokes. Cover and bake in a 375 degree oven for 40 minutes or until chicken is tender. Serves 4.

Carol Brown
Solon, Iowa

## MRS. KMET'S CHICKEN

2      cans French-style green beans
1      can cream of mushroom soup
6      boned chicken breasts
6      slices boiled ham
1/2   cup melted butter
1/2   cup sherry
       garlic powder
       paprika

In a 9x13-inch baking dish layer drained beans and then the soup. Make a pocket in each chicken breast half and stuff with a slice of ham, securing with a toothpick. Place breasts on top of soup. Drizzle with melted butter and sherry. Sprinkle garlic powder and paprika on top to taste. Bake uncovered 1 hour in a 350 degree oven.

*This is delicious served with my mother's "Brown Rice". (See Vegetables and Side Dishes.)*

Cynthia Hubbard Shive
Iowa City, Iowa

# CHICKEN IBO

| | |
|---|---|
| 3 | **whole chicken breasts or 6 large halves** |
| 1/2 | **teaspoon salt** |
| 1/4 | **teaspoon pepper** |
| 1/4 | **cup flour** |
| 1/4 | **cup butter, divided** |
| 2 | **large onions, chopped** |
| 1 | **cup chopped fresh mushrooms** |
| 2 | **tablespoons butter** |
| 2 | **tablespoons flour** |
| 1 | **cup milk** |
| 1/4 | **teaspoon salt** |
| 1/2 | **cup cream sherry** |
| 1/2 | **teaspoon nutmeg** |
| 1 | **cup cashews** |

Remove skin from chicken breasts, bone chicken and cut meat in 1-1/2 by 1-1/2-inch pieces. Season the chicken pieces with the salt and pepper and coat them with the flour. Heat 2 tablespoons butter in a large frying pan over medium heat and brown the chicken pieces until they are golden. When they are browned, remove from frying pan and set them aside in a 13x9-inch casserole.

Heat remainder of butter in the frying pan in which the chicken was cooked. Add the onions and mushrooms and saute until they are cooked through, but not browned. Turn off heat and leave the mixture in the pan while you make the white sauce.

*White sauce:* Make by melting the 2 tablespoons butter in a saucepan. Add flour and mix well to form a paste. Over low heat add milk all at once and stir constantly until the sauce boils and thickens. Remove from heat and stir in 1/4 teaspoon salt.

Add the white sauce, sherry and nutmeg to the onion-mushroom mixture and mix well. Pour this sauce over the browned chicken pieces and mix well. Bake uncovered at 350 degrees for 30 minutes. Just before serving, add the cashews and mix well. Serves 6.

*This recipe can be made the day before. Take it out of the refrigerator 1/2 hour before baking and add 10 minutes to the baking time.*

Carol Brandt
Newport News, Virginia

# KING RANCH KITCHEN CASSEROLE

| | |
|---|---|
| 1 | 3 to 4 pound package of chicken breasts |
| | water to cover chicken |
| 1 | dozen frozen tortillas |
| 1 | can cream of mushroom soup |
| 1 | cup chopped green pepper |
| 1 | cup chopped onion |
| 1 | tablespoon chili powder |
| 3/4 | pound grated Cheddar cheese |
| 10 | ounces canned tomatoes, mashed |
| 1 | can Rotel tomatoes, mashed |

Boil chicken breasts until tender. Reserve stock. Remove chicken from bone and dice meat. Line bottom and sides of greased 3-quart casserole dish with a layer of 6 tortillas. Sprinkle with 2 tablespoons chicken stock. Make a layer of 1 can undiluted mushroom soup, half of the diced chicken and half of the peppers, onions and chili powder. Cover with remaining tortillas. Sprinkle with chicken stock and repeat layers as above. Top last layer with cheese and mixture of canned and Rotel tomatoes. Cover with aluminum foil and bake at 350 degrees for one hour. Serves 8.

*Serve with tossed green salad and hot French bread.*

Susan Burke
Broken Arrow, Oklahoma

# CHICKEN PARADISE

| | |
|---|---|
| 12 | slices bacon |
| 1 | package dried beef sandwich slices |
| 12 | deboned and skinned chicken breasts |
| | salt and pepper to taste |
| | seasoned salt to taste |
| 2 | cans cream of chicken soup |
| 1 | 16-ounce carton sour cream |
| 1 | 8-ounce package cream cheese, softened |

Fry bacon until half done. Line a large rectangular baking dish with the beef slices. Wrap bacon around each chicken breast and place on beef slices. Sprinkle the salts and pepper on each breast. Mix together the soup, sour cream and cream cheese. Spread over chicken. Place the covered casserole in a 350 degree oven and bake 1 hour. Remove cover and continue baking for an additional 30 minutes. Makes 8 to 10 servings.

*Rice is good with this dish. The chicken casserole can be made ahead of time; frozen and reheated!*

Sandy Dabney
Dallas, Texas

## APPLE CHICKEN

| | |
|---|---|
| 4 | boned, split chicken breasts |
| 2 | tablespoons flour |
| | salt and pepper to taste |
| 2 | tablespoons butter |
| 2 | Golden Delicious apples, chopped |
| 2 | tablespoons butter |
| 1 | tablespoon sugar |
| 1 | tablespoon sherry |
| 1 | cup heavy cream |
| 2 | tablespoons finely chopped parsley |

Roll the chicken in flour, salt and pepper; melt butter in saute pan and brown chicken, lowering heat and cooking chicken until done and juices run clear. Remove pieces from pan and keep warm. Add chopped apples and 2 tablespoons butter to pan, sprinkle with sugar and cook, stirring until barely soft, about 5 minutes. Place apples on chicken and keep warm. Prepare sauce by adding sherry and cream to pan and cook, stirring until cream is reduced and thickened. Pour sauce over chicken and sprinkle with parsley. Serves 4.

*Can be kept warm for 20 minutes in a 140 degree oven if needed. I use an ovenproof platter, so chicken and apples can go directly from pan to serving dish. Since things at Keystone cool quickly, warm plates help!*

Meryl O. Dun
San Anselmo, California

## SUPER CHICKEN

| | |
|---|---|
| 5 | whole, cooked chicken breasts |
| 3 | boxes frozen French-cut green beans |
| 2 | cans cream of chicken soup |
| 1 | soup can mayonnaise |
| 1 | cup sherry |
| | Parmesan cheese |

Skin and cut chicken into large pieces. Place in the bottom of a 9x13-inch baking dish. Mix beans, soup, mayonnaise and sherry and pour over chicken. Sprinkle liberally with Parmesan cheese and bake uncovered in a 325 degree oven for 40 minutes. Serves 6.

Dorris Davis
Webster Groves, Missouri

## SUPER SIMPLE CHICKEN BREASTS WITH CHIPPED BEEF

| 5 | whole chicken breasts, split, skinned and boned |
| 1/2 | pound bacon |
| 6-8 | ounces dried chipped beef |
| 3 | cans cream of mushroom soup |
| 3 | 8-ounce cartons sour cream |

Wrap each boned chicken breast diagonally with bacon. Cover the bottom of a 9x13x2-inch baking dish with chipped beef. Placed chicken breasts on chipped beef. Mix together mushroom soup and sour cream. Pour over chicken. Bake uncovered in a preheated 275 degree oven for 3-1/2 to 4 hours or until chicken is tender. Makes 8 to 10 servings.

*If chipped beef is very salty, rinse and drain. The sauce is good on wild rice as an accompaniment. Tastes like pheasant!*

Barbara N. O'Hara
Dayton, Ohio

## BASTARD BARBEQUE CHICKEN

whole chicken breasts, halved
garlic salt or garlic powder
butter
brown sugar

Place chicken breasts in casserole dish or baking pan. Sprinkle generously with garlic salt or powder. Dot surface liberally with good-sized pats of butter. Pack well with brown sugar using your hands to pack and fill all crevices to fill baking pan. Bake in a preheated 350 degree oven until done, at least 1 hour. May crisp lightly under the broiler.

*This was always a hit at my dinner parties in Craneridge, New York.*

Pat Hubbard
Keystone, Colorado

# SOUR CREAM MIX ENCHILADAS CASSEROLE

| 2 | pints sour cream |
|---|---|
| 1 | cup milk |
| 2 | cans cream of chicken soup |
| 1 | small onion, chopped |
| 2 | cans mild chopped green chilies |
| 2 | cups finely chopped cooked chicken |
| 1 | package soft tortillas |
| 2 | pounds longhorn cheese, grated |

Mix sour cream, milk, soup, onion and chilies in a saucepan. Heat slowly and add chicken. Put a small amount of sauce on the bottom of a greased 9x13-inch pan. Layer tortillas over sauce, and continue layering with sauce and tortillas, topping with the cheese. Bake in a preheated 350 degree oven for 45 minutes.

*These enchiladas may be frozen. Defrost 8 hours before baking. This casserole is delicious as a brunch or dinner entree.*

Sandy Dabney
Dallas, Texas


# PRIME RIB

Place rib roast in open shallow pan, ribs down. Start with cold oven. Roast at 350 degrees for 1 hour. Turn oven completely off and leave meat in oven with door closed. (Do not open door to peek!) Leave for at least 3 hours.

Insert meat thermometer and roast at 350 degrees until thermometer reads desired degree of pink in center. (Medium rare center will take about 1 hour.)

Do not season until cooking is complete.

*This is a very dependable recipe regardless of the size of the roast.*

Aaron Parkhurst, M.D.
Greeley, Colorado

# BEEF NAPOLEON

| | |
|---|---|
| 1/2 | cup flour |
| 2 | 2-pound beef tenderloin roasts |
| 1/4 | cup flour |
| 1/2 | teaspoon salt |
| 1/2 | teaspoon pepper |
| 1/2 | cup cooking oil |
| 1/4 | cup diced onion |
| 1/4 | cup diced celery |
| 1/4 | cup diced carrot |
| 2 | tablespoons tomato paste |
| 2 | 10-ounce cans condensed beef broth |
| 1/2 | cup sherry |

Sprinkle 1/2 cup flour in an 8x8-inch pan. Bake in oven at 350 degrees for 30 minutes until flour is lightly browned. Shake pan occasionally to mix flour. Coat meat with mixture of 1/4 cup unbrowned flour, salt and pepper. Brown meat quickly in oil over high heat in a large skillet. Remove meat to a rack in a shallow roasting pan. Reserve drippings in the skillet.

Cook onion, celery and carrot in drippings about 4 minutes. Blend in browned flour and tomato paste. Add beef broth. Cook and stir until bubbly and thickened. Add sherry; remove from heat.

Pour sauce over meat. Roast uncovered in oven at 425 degrees for 45 minutes, or until meat thermometer registers 140 degrees for rare. Transfer meat to a serving platter; spoon sauce over each roast. Serves 8.

Carol Brandt
Newport News, Virginia

61

## WESTERN BARBEQUE BRISKET

| 1 | 5 to 7 pound beef brisket |
| | celery salt |
| | garlic powder |
| | salt |
| | Worcestershire sauce |
| 1/3 | cup Liquid Smoke |

Using a knife, punch holes all the way through both sides of brisket. Liberally sprinkle meat, fat side up, with celery salt, garlic powder, salt, Worcestershire sauce and Liquid Smoke. Cover with foil and marinate 12 hours in refrigerator. Turn meat in pan, re-cover and marinate for an additional 12 hours. Cook 6 hours in a 250 degree oven. Pour off and save juices in gravy boat. Slice beef and place on platter. Serve with the juices.

Patti Kimple
Dallas, Texas

## BARBEQUE FOR A CROWD

| 1 | 4 to 5 pound chuck roast |
| 1 | bunch celery, chopped |
| 1 | large onion, chopped |
| 1 | 20-ounce bottle of ketchup |
| 1 | 12-ounce bottle chili sauce |
| 1 | teaspoon black pepper |
| 1 | tablespoon salt |

Combine roast and all ingredients in large pot. Simmer on low heat for 4 hours, cooking until meat falls from the bone or extremely well done. Shred meat with fork and place in second pot. Add enough sauce to reach consistency desired.

*Serve on hamburger buns or rolls of your choice. Remaining sauce may be frozen.*

Dorothy Bennett
Iowa City, Iowa

## BARBEQUED SHORT RIBS

1     large bottle barbeque sauce
1     can beer
3-5   pounds short ribs

Combine barbeque sauce and beer. Place meat in large baking dish and brush with mixture. Bake covered in 350 degree oven for 4 hours.

*Very good served with fettucini.*

Joanne Manion
St. Louis, Missouri

## FLANK STEAK MARINADE

     flank steak
1     large bottle French dressing

Place flank steak in large zip-locking bag and cover with French dressing. Seal bag and allow to marinate overnight. Drain meat and save excess dressing and use to brush meat when barbecuing.

*Delicious, and meat will be very tender!*

Michael Shive
Overland Park, Kansas

## MADE RITES

| 1 | cup water |
| 1 | large onion, chopped |
| 1 | teaspoon chili powder |
| 1/4 | cup catsup |
| 2 | pounds lean ground beef |
| 1 | tablespoon prepared mustard |
| | salt and pepper to taste |

In large saucepan combine first 4 ingredients. Bring to boil and cook 10 minutes, stirring occasionally. Add ground beef and mustard. Cook, stirring to break up meat until meat is done. Freezes well.

*Makes great sandwiches served with dill slices.*

Jane Bergman
Cedar Rapids, Iowa

## BROWNIE'S BURGERS

| 2 | pounds lean ground beef |
| 1/3 | cup chopped green pepper |
| 1/3 | cup chopped onion |
| 2 | teaspoons Worcestershire sauce |
| 1 | teaspoon garlic salt |
| 4 | drops Tabasco sauce |
| 1 | teaspoon oregano |
| 2 | tablespoons soy sauce |

Thoroughly mix together all ingredients and shape into patties. Fry in lightly-greased skillet or grill over hot coals. Serve medium to medium-rare on hamburger buns.

Dave Brown
Coralville, Iowa

# SUNNY'S CHINESE DISH

| | |
|---|---|
| 1-1/2 | pounds round steak |
| 1/2 | cup soy sauce |
| 1 | teaspoon sugar |
| 3 | large tomatoes, peeled |
| 2 | green peppers, seeded |
| 1/4 | cup salad oil |
| 1 | clove garlic, crushed |
| 3/4 | teaspoon ginger |
| 2 | teaspoons cornstarch |
| 2 | teaspoons soy sauce |

Cut round steak across the grain in paper thin strips. This is easier to do if meat is partially frozen. Place the meat in a bowl and pour over it a mixture of 1/2 cup soy sauce and 1 teaspoon sugar. Let it marinate for 30 minutes, turning the meat after the first 15 minutes. Meanwhile, cut tomatoes into 8 wedges and cut peppers into narrow strips 1-1/2 inches in length. In a large skillet, heat salad oil. Add garlic and ginger and cook for 3 to 4 minutes. Remove the garlic. Add green pepper and saute, stirring constantly for 3 minutes. Then add the beef and its liquid and cook for another 3 minutes.

Add tomatoes and cover. Simmer until tomatoes are hot. Blend cornstarch with remaining soy sauce. Gently stir into mixture and cook 1 more minute. Remove from heat. Serves 6.

*Serve with fluffy rice garnished with garden peas and a tossed green salad.*

Sunny McNall
Cedar Rapids, Iowa

# ORIENTAL BEEF STEAK STRIPS

| 2 | pounds round steak |
| 2 | tablespoons cooking oil |
|   | water |
| 1/3 | cup soy sauce |
| 2 | teaspoons sugar |
| 1/4 | teaspoon pepper |
| 1 | clove garlic, minced |
| 3 | carrots |
| 2 | green peppers, cut in 1-inch squares |
| 8 | green onions, cut in 1-1/2-inch pieces |
| 1/2 | pound fresh mushrooms, halved |
| 2 | tablespoons cornstarch |
| 1/4 | cup water |
|   | cooked rice |

Cut round steak into strips 1/8-inch thick or thinner and 3 to
4 inches long. Brown meat in cooking oil. Pour off drippings
and combine with water to make 1 cup. Add soy sauce, sugar,
pepper and garlic and add to meat. Cover and cook slowly 45
minutes. Using vegetable parer, cut carrots lengthwise into
thin strips and cut strips in half. Add carrots, pepper, onion
and mushrooms to meat; cover and continue cooking 15 minutes. Combine cornstarch and water and use to thicken cooking liquid for gravy. Serve with cooked rice. Makes 6 to 8
servings.

Debbie Haynes
Merriam, Kansas

# ITALIAN BEEF

| 1 | 6 to 8 pound beef round, rump or very lean chuck roast |
| 3 | garlic cloves, slivered |
| 2 | cups chopped onions |
| 1/2 | jar mild cherry peppers, chopped |
| 1/3 | cup vinegar |
| 3 | cups water |
| 1 | tablespoon oregano leaves |
| 1 | bay leaf |
|   | salt and pepper to taste |

Stud meat with garlic cloves. Bake uncovered in a 350 degree
oven until medium-rare, approximately 1-1/2 to 2 hours. Cool
and slice thinly. Return meat to juices in pan.
Add remaining ingredients. Cover and bake at 275 degrees at
least 3 more hours, stirring occasionally.

*Serve on crusty rolls. The juice is delicious. Seems to taste bet-
ter if made a day or two in advance. It freezes well.*

Annette Fricke
Monticello, Illinois

# FAJITAS

2 pounds skirt, fajita or flank steak
2 limes
4 cloves garlic, pressed
 black pepper to taste
1 can Lone Star Beer (Texas)
4 ounces olive oil
 fresh flour tortillas
 salsa fresca a la Mexicana
 guacamole
 cheese
 sour cream

Marinate fajita steak 24 hours in the marinade of juice from limes, garlic, pepper, beer and oil. Cook steak medium rare on barbeque pit. Serve with fresh flour tortillas and condiments of salsa fresca a la Mexicana, guacamole, cheese and sour cream. Makes 8 servings.

*It is important to cut steaks against the grain in small strips, place in tortilla with condiments, fold over and enjoy.*

O. B. Jackson, Jr. M.D.
Austin, Texas

# CABBAGE ROLLS

1/2 cup rice
1-1/4 cups milk
3/4 pound ground beef
1/4 pound ground pork
1 can condensed bouillon, mixed with 1 can of water
2 teaspoons salt
1/4 teaspoon pepper
1 medium-sized head of cabbage
2 tablespoons brown sugar
2 tablespoons butter

Cook rice with milk in double boiler for 10 minutes. Add meat, 1 cup bouillon (mixed with water) and salt and pepper. Continue cooking until rice is soft, 10 to 15 minutes. Remove leaves from head of cabbage and put in boiling salted water. Cook 2 minutes and drain. Spoon meat mixture onto each leaf, roll and fasten with toothpick. Arrange in 2-quart baking dish; sprinkle with brown sugar. Add remaining bouillon and butter. Cover and simmer 25 to 30 minutes, adding water if necessary. Serves 6.

Scoble Gallery
Keystone Resort

# SPAGHETTI PIE

| | |
|---|---|
| 12 | ounces spaghetti |
| 1/2 | cup butter |
| 1 | cup freshly grated Parmesan cheese |
| 3 | eggs, well beaten |
| 2-1/2 | pounds ground beef |
| 1 | cup finely chopped onion |
| 2 | 15-ounce cans tomato sauce |
| 2 | 6-ounce cans tomato paste |
| 2 | teaspoons sugar |
| 1/3 | cup water |
| 1 | tablespoon oregano |
| | garlic salt |
| | basil |
| | salt |
| 2 | cups sour cream |
| 8 | ounces shredded mozzarella cheese |

Cook spaghetti al dente; drain. Stir in butter, Parmesan cheese and eggs. Chop well with knife and fork; form into a "crust" in two buttered 10-inch pie tins. Let cool. Cook ground beef and onion; drain off fat. Stir in tomato sauce and paste, sugar and water. Add oregano, garlic salt, basil and salt to taste. Heat thoroughly. Spread sour cream on bottom of spaghetti "crusts". Fill pies with meat sauce. Cover with cheese. Bake at 350 degrees for 30 minutes. Serves 12.

*May be frozen.*

Kathleen Chott
Western Springs, Illinois

## EL DORADO CASSEROLE

|       | oil for frying |
|-------|----------------|
| 1/2   | small onion, chopped |
| 1     | pound ground beef |
| 1     | package taco seasoning |
| 1     | 6-ounce jar tomato paste |
| 1     | 2-ounce jar Jalapeno peppers |
| 1     | 6-ounce can black olives |
| 1     | 16-ounce carton sour cream |
| 1     | 12-ounce bag Fritos Corn Chips |
| 1/2   | pound shredded Cheddar cheese |

Put oil in skillet and cook chopped onion until clear. Add ground beef. Cook until just brown and drain excess fat. In saucepan mix taco seasoning according to package with tomato paste. Add onion and meat mixture. Set aside. In another bowl combine drained and chopped Jalapenos, drained and chopped black olives and sour cream. In greased 1-1/2-quart-sized casserole layer the Fritos on bottom. Pour taco and meat sauce over chips. Spread sour cream mixture as next layer and then grated cheese on the top. Bake 20 to 35 minutes in a 375 degree oven until mixture is heated through.

Kathy Mickalson
Iowa City, Iowa

## EASY ONE-STEP LASAGNA

| 2 | pounds lean ground beef |
|---|-------------------------|
| 1 | 32-ounce container spaghetti sauce |
| 1 | 24-ounce carton ricotta or cottage cheese |
| 2 | eggs |
| 1 | 16-ounce package lasagna noodles (uncooked) |
| 1 | pound mozzarella cheese, grated |

Brown ground beef and add sauce until heated. Combine ricotta (or cottage) cheese and eggs. Spoon one-third of the meat sauce into a 9x13-inch pan. Cover with single layer of noodles. Spoon half of ricotta cheese mixture over noodles. Cover with another third of meat sauce; then half the mozzarella, noodles, rest of ricotta mixture, meat sauce and mozzarella. Cover loosely with foil. Bake at 350 degrees for 1-1/2 hours.

Thom Davis
Grand Mound, Iowa

# LASAGNA

| | |
|---|---|
| 12 | ounces lasagna noodles |
| 2 | pounds ground beef |
| 4 | tablespoons olive oil |
| 2 | cloves garlic |
| 1 | onion, chopped |
| 2 | 6-ounce cans tomato paste |
| 2 | 8-ounce cans tomato sauce |
| 3/4 | cup water |
| | salt and pepper to taste |
| | Italian seasoning |
| 2 | eggs |
| 1/2 | cup Parmesan cheese |
| 2 | teaspoons salt |
| 1/2 | teaspoon pepper |
| 1/4 | cup parsley flakes |
| 1 | pound mozzarella cheese, shredded |
| 1/2 | pound Monterey Jack cheese, shredded |
| 1 | pint ricotta cheese |

Cook noodles until tender, cool in water. Brown meat in olive oil and add garlic, onion, tomato paste, tomato sauce, water, salt, pepper and Italian seasoning. Simmer meat sauce for 45 minutes. Combine eggs, Parmesan cheese, salt, pepper and parsley flakes together in mixing bowl. In a greased 8x14-inch baking dish layer one-third of the meat sauce, half the noodles, one-third of the Parmesan cheese mixture, one-third mozzarella, Monterey Jack and ricotta cheeses; repeat. Complete with remaining meat sauce and cheeses. Bake at 350 degrees for 35 minutes. Remove from oven and let stand a few minutes before serving. Makes 10 to 12 servings.

Berniece Brekke
Littleton, Colorado

# EASY LASAGNA

| | |
|---|---|
| 1 | pound lean ground beef |
| 1 | cup chopped onion |
| 3 | cloves garlic, chopped |
| 4 | cups tomato juice |
| 2 | cups sliced mushrooms |
| 1 | 6-ounce can tomato paste |
| 1 | teaspoon oregano |
| 1 | teaspoon salt |
| 1/8 | teaspoon pepper |
| 8 | ounces lasagna noodles, uncooked |
| 1 | 15-ounce carton ricotta cheese |
| 2 | cups (8 ounces) shredded mozzarella cheese |
| 1-1/2 | cups grated Parmesan or Romano cheese |
| 1 | teaspoon parsley flakes |

*A little sauce in the pan first keeps the noodles from sticking. This is a super simple way to make lasagna because the noodles are not pre-boiled before assembling the dish!*

Brown meat, onion and garlic. Pour off any fat. Stir in tomato juice, mushrooms, tomato paste, oregano, and salt and pepper. Simmer 30 minutes, stirring occasionally. Preheat oven to 350 degrees. In a greased 9x13 inch casserole, layer half each of noodles, sauce, ricotta, mozzarella and Parmesan cheese. Repeat. Top with parsley. Cover with foil and bake 30 minutes. Uncover and bake 15 minutes longer. Remove from oven and let stand 10 minutes before cutting. Serves 6 to 8.

Annette Fricke
Monticello, Illinois

# BEEF AND WILD RICE CASSEROLE

| | |
|---|---|
| 2 | pounds ground beef |
| 3 | large onions, diced |
| 3 | stalks celery, diced |
| 2 | cans mushroom soup |
| 2 | soup cans water |
| 1 | large can mushrooms and liquid |
| 1 | cup wild rice |
| 1 | tablespoon soy sauce |
| | salt to taste |

Brown meat and onions. Add remaining ingredients except soy sauce. Bake at 350 degrees, 1-1/2 hours. Stir about every half hour. If dry, add another can of mushroom soup and half can of water. When done, add soy sauce and salt to taste. Serves 12 to 14.

Pat Grossman
Wayzata, Minnesota


# CRUSTY BEEF, CHEESE AND NOODLE CASSEROLE

| | |
|---|---|
| 2 | tablespoons vegetable oil |
| 1 | onion, chopped |
| 2 | pounds ground beef |
| 4 | 10-1/4-ounce cans meatless spaghetti sauce |
| 1 | teaspoon salt |
| 1 | pound fine noodles, cooked and drained |
| 1 | pound sharp Cheddar cheese, grated |
| | seasoning salt to taste |

Heat oil and cook onion to a golden brown. Add meat and stir just until it has lost its red color and add sauce and salt. In a 9x12-inch baking pan make layers beginning with noodles, then sauce and cheese. Repeat. Bake in preheated 350 degree oven for 1 hour.

Dorothy Bennett
Iowa City, Iowa

## DAY-BEFORE MAZZETTI CASSEROLE

| | |
|---|---|
| 2 | pounds ground beef |
| 2-1/2 | cups chopped celery with tops |
| 2 | cups chopped onion |
| 1 | tablespoon water |
| 1 | 8-ounce package medium-wide noodles |
| 2 | cans cream of tomato soup |
| 1 | 6-ounce can mushrooms with juice |
| 2 | tablespoons salt |
| 1/2 | teaspoon pepper |
| 1/2 | pound sharp Cheddar cheese, grated |

In frying pan, brown the ground beef and drain. Add to beef the celery, onion and water. Cover and steam until vegetables are tender. In large saucepan, cook package of noodles as directed and drain. Add the ground beef mixture plus the tomato soup, mushrooms and seasonings. Mix together thoroughly and pour into a 3-quart casserole. Sprinkle with the grated Cheddar cheese. Cover and refrigerate for 24 hours. When ready to bake, put into a cold oven and turn on to 250 degrees. Bake uncovered for 1 hour or until bubbly. Serves 8 to 10.

Betty Oglesby
Iowa City, Iowa

## PORK ROAST WITH LEMON OR "PORC AU CITRON"

| | |
|---|---|
| 2 | lemons |
| 1-1/2 | pounds pork roast |
| 1 | tablespoon oil |
| 1 | tablespoon Dijon mustard |
| 1 | clove garlic, minced |
| 1 | teaspoon lemon juice |
| 1/2 | teaspoon salt |
| 2 | dashes white pepper |
| 1 | cup cream |
| | cornstarch if needed |

Carefully peel one lemon. Cut peel into about 25 small pieces and insert all over meat. Combine oil, mustard, garlic, lemon juice, salt and pepper. Pour over meat and let marinate in refrigerator for at least 1 hour. Remove marinated meat from the refrigerator 1 hour before cooking, so that the marinade will adhere better. Place roast in ovenproof dish and bake in a 425 degree oven for 30 minutes, basting once or twice. Remove meat from dish and keep hot. Add cream to meat juices in ovenproof dish and heat thoroughly in oven. You may thicken sauce, if needed, with a little cornstarch. Cut roast into slices, pour sauce over and garnish with lemon slices.

Barbara Cornelsen
Geneva, Switzerland

# PORK CHOP CASSEROLE

| | |
|---|---|
| 4 | pork chops |
| | salt and pepper to taste |
| 4 | heaping tablespoons raw rice |
| 1 | 16-ounce can whole tomatoes |
| 1 | large onion |
| | sugar |
| 1/2 | teaspoon rosemary |
| 1 | bay leaf |
| | water or tomato juice |

Salt and pepper both sides of 4 raw, unbrowned pork chops, and place in baking dish. Spoon a heaping tablespoon of raw rice on each chop and pour a little juice from the can of tomatoes over rice. Place a thick slice of onion over rice on each pork chop. Pour can of tomatoes over chops. Sprinkle with a dash of sugar, rosemary and crumbled bay leaf. Be sure there is enough liquid to fully cook rice—rice should be covered with liquid. Add water or tomato juice. Cover tightly and bake in a preheated 350 degree oven for 2 hours.

Robert W. Younghusband
Dillon, Colorado

# SPINACH AND HAM STRATA

| | |
|---|---|
| 4 | cups cubed bread (white or whole wheat) |
| 1 | cup shredded American cheese |
| 10 | ounce package frozen chopped spinach (thawed and drained) |
| 1 | cup cubed ham |
| 1 | cup shredded Swiss cheese |
| 4 | eggs |
| 2 | cups milk |
| 1 | tablespoon chopped onion |
| 1 | tablespoon dry mustard |
| 1-1/2 | teaspoons salt (optional) |
| 1/4 | teaspoon pepper |

In a 9-inch square baking dish, layer half of the bread cubes, then American cheese, spinach, ham, Swiss cheese and remaining bread crumbs. In a separate bowl combine the eggs, milk and remaining ingredients. Blend well and gently pour over casserole. Cover and refrigerate overnight (or at least 1 hour). Bake in a preheated 350 degree oven for 50 to 60 minutes. (One check is to insert a knife in the middle and if it comes out "clean" the strata is set!) Let stand for 5 minutes before serving.

*Great "make-ahead"!*

Elra Currie
Belleaire Bluffs, Florida

# DAD SHIVE'S FAVORITE BOILED DINNER

| | |
|---|---|
| 1 | 3 to 4 pound smoked pork butt |
| 2 | bay leaves |
| | black peppercorns |
| | carrots |
| | potatoes, peeled |
| 1 | head cabbage |
| | green beans |
| | white vinegar |

*On my first trip to Keystone, I made this meal for my future in-laws (my husband proposed only that afternoon). It is very simple and great for after skiing—it now has become a regular.*

Place meat in a large soup kettle and cover with cold water. Add bay leaves and sprinkle with black peppercorns. Cook over medium heat, covered, for 2 hours. After 1 hour, add carrots and potatoes, cover and continue to simmer. Fifteen minutes prior to serving, quarter cabbage and place on top with green beans; cover and steam. To serve, drain vegetables and potatoes, arrange on outside of serving platter. Drain meat and place in the middle of platter. Serve with a cruet of white vinegar to be sprinkled over cabbage, potatoes and meat.

Cynthia Hubbard Shive
Iowa City, Iowa

## SAUSAGE STROGANOFF

| | |
|---|---|
| 1 | pound bulk sausage |
| 1 | cup finely chopped onion |
| 1 | cup finely chopped green pepper |
| 1 | 1-pound can tomatoes |
| 1 | cup sour cream |
| 1 | cup water |
| 1 | teaspoon sugar |
| 1/2 | teaspoon salt |
| 1/2 | teaspoon chili powder |
| 1 | cup raisins |
| 1 | 6-ounce package egg noodles, cooked |

In large frying pan, break up sausage and brown, draining fat as it accumulates. Add onion and green pepper and cook with sausage until onions are clear. Combine remaining ingredients except noodles in separate bowl and add to browned sausage in pan. Stir in noodles. Keep warm over low heat until serving or place in a 9x9-inch casserole in a 250 degree oven for up to 1 hour. Serves 4.

Gorsuch Ltd.                                          Keystone Resort

## SAUSAGE BRUNCH

| | |
|---|---|
| 1-1/2 | pounds pork sausage |
| 9 | eggs |
| 3 | cups milk |
| 1-1/2 | teaspoons dry mustard |
| 1 | teaspoon salt |
| 3 | slices cubed bread |
| 1-1/2 | cups grated Colby or Cheddar cheese |
| 1/2 | pound fresh mushrooms |

Brown and drain the sausage. Mix with remaining ingredients and refrigerate covered overnight. Bake uncovered for 1 hour in a preheated 350 degree oven.

Sue Bahle                                          St. Louis, Missouri

# LAMB SHANKS

| | |
|---|---|
| 4 | lamb shanks |
| 2 | tablespoons lemon juice |
| 1/2 | teaspoon garlic powder |
| 1 | cup all-purpose flour |
| 2 | teaspoons salt |
| 1/2 | teaspoon pepper |
| 1/2 | cup salad oil |
| 1 | 10-1/2-ounce can condensed beef broth, undiluted |
| 1 | cup water |
| 1/2 | cup dry vermouth |
| 2 | medium onions, quartered |
| 4 | carrots, peeled, and cut into serving pieces |
| 4 | stalks celery, cut into serving pieces |

Rub lamb with lemon juice and garlic powder, set aside for 20 minutes. Combine flour, salt and pepper in a plastic bag; shake shanks one at a time to coat with flour. Save flour. Brown shanks in hot oil in large heavy skillet. Remove meat from pan. Add 4 tablespoons of the seasoned flour to pan drippings, stir and brown the flour. Add beef broth, water and vermouth and stir, cooking until slightly thickened. Add onions. Place shanks in large baking dish and pour the broth mixture over them. Shanks should be in one layer. Refrigerate.

When ready to bake, place in 350 degree oven, uncovered, for 1-1/2 hours. Turn shanks, add carrots and celery and continue to bake 1 more hour.

*The gravy is very good over egg noodles.*

Elra Currie
Belleaire Bluffs, Florida

# SWISS CHEESE PIE

| | |
|---|---|
| 1 | pastry for 8-inch pie |
| 2 | slices bacon, cut into 1/4-inch pieces |
| 2 | tablespoons finely chopped onion |
| 1 | cup milk |
| 1/2 | cup whipping cream |
| 3 | tablespoons cornstarch |
| 3 | tablespoons milk |
| 3 | eggs |
| 1/8 | teaspoon nutmeg |
| 1/2 | teaspoon salt |
| | dash white pepper |
| 1-1/2 | cups shredded Swiss cheese |

Heat oven to 400 degrees. Prepare pastry for 1 pie crust. Fit into greased 8-inch pie plate; trim edge. Prick with fork. Cook bacon over medium heat until limp. Add onion; cook and stir until onion is tender but not brown. Set aside. Heat 1 cup milk and the cream in saucepan over low heat. Mix cornstarch and 3 tablespoons milk; stir into milk and cream mixture. Cook, stirring constantly, until sauce is smooth and thick. Remove from heat and cool slightly. Beat eggs until light and fluffy. Brush about 1 tablespoon beaten egg on pastry. Mix nutmeg, salt, pepper, cheese and the cooked cream sauce into eggs. Stir in bacon and onions (with any fat that is in the pan). Mix and turn into pastry-lined pan. Bake on top rack of oven until nicely browned, about 35 minutes. Serves 6 to 8.

*The pie will shrink as it cools. It can be served piping hot, warm or cold. The pie can be made in advance; cooked completely, cooled, wrapped securely in aluminum foil and frozen. To reheat, place foil-wrapped frozen pie in 350 degree oven and heat until hot, about 1 hour. This is a quiche that freezes and travels very well.*

Donna Blair
Saratoga, California

## TEXAS QUICHE

1      prepared 9-inch pie crust
1      cup grated Cheddar cheese
1      cup grated Monterey Jack cheese
3      eggs
1      teaspoon salt
1/4      teaspoon pepper
1      teaspoon chili powder
1      4-ounce can green chilies
1      12-1/4-ounce can ripe olives (chopped)
1-1/2    cups half and half or canned milk

Heat oven to 350 degrees. Spread grated cheeses in pie crust. Mix eggs, salt, pepper, chili powder, chilies, olives and half and half. Pour over cheese. Bake 45 to 55 minutes or until knife inserted in center comes out clean.

*Great also as an appetizer. Very quick and simple.*

Susan Burke
Broken Arrow, Oklahoma

## PUFFY FONDUE

1/2      cup butter
12      slices bread, crusts removed
1      pound sharp Cheddar cheese, sliced
4      eggs
1      quart milk
1      teaspoon salt
1      teaspoon dry mustard
       dash of cayenne pepper
       paprika

Butter the bread slices. Place six slices on the bottom of a buttered 9x13-inch pan. Top each slice with cheese. Cover with remaining bread. Combine eggs, milk, salt, dry mustard and cayenne pepper in mixer and blend. Pour mixture over cheese sandwiches. Sprinkle with paprika. Cover and refrigerate overnight. Bake uncovered at 350 degreees until puffed, about 45 minutes. Serves 6.

Pat Grossman
Wayzata, Minnesota

# PERU CREEK OMELET FOR TWO

| 1/2 | medium onion |
| 1 | cup chopped broccoli |
| 1 | green pepper |
| | butter |
| 1/4 | cup wine |
| 1/2 | pound fresh mushrooms |
| 1 | medium tomato |
| 3 | tablespoons Grey Poupon mustard |
| 1/2 | cup sour cream or yogurt |
| 6 | eggs |
| 1/4 | cup milk |
| | dash salt |
| | dash lemon pepper |
| 1 | cup grated cheese (your favorite) |
| | paprika |

Chop vegetables into small pieces. Add onions, broccoli and green pepper to melted butter in pan with 1/4 cup of wine; saute 5 minutes on medium heat. Add mushrooms and saute for 5 more minutes. Add next 3 ingredients and simmer until thickened. Set aside on low heat.

Melt butter in omelet pan. Mix together eggs, milk, salt and pepper until frothy, in a blender. Pour into omelet pan, pre-heated on medium high heat; cook omelet, lifting edges to allow uncooked portion on top to run off onto pan until firm.

Add one-third of the vegetables you sauteed and flip edge of omelet. Slide out onto serving dish. Cover with remaining vegetables and grated cheese. Garnish with paprika.

*Use heated salsa, sour cream or guacamole as condiments. This is my husband Tom's special recipe for Sunday brunch. We love to share it with visiting friends and our Summit County friends and relatives. The "Spring Fling" (see Beverages) is a great "twist" to add to the meal—Karen Putts.*

La Cima          Keystone Resort

# CHEESE ENCHILADAS

| | |
|---|---|
| 1/2 | medium onion, chopped |
| 1/2 | green pepper, chopped |
| 5 | Jalapeno peppers, chopped |
| 2 | cloves garlic, crushed |
| 1 | tablespoon olive oil |
| 1 | 16-ounce can tomato sauce |
| 2 | tomatoes, chopped |
| 1/2 | teaspoon crushed cumin seed |
| | pinch oregano |
| 2 | teaspoons sugar |
| 1 | tablespoon lemon juice |
| 8 | flour tortillas |
| 1 | pound Cheddar cheese, grated |
| 1 | pint sour cream |
| | sliced black olives |

In frying pan saute onion, green pepper, Jalapeno peppers and garlic cloves in olive oil. Add next 6 ingredients and simmer 20 minutes while preparing tortillas. Quickly fry tortillas in hot oil, both sides, one by one. Fill each with grated Cheddar cheese. Roll up and place in 9x13-inch baking pan. Cover with sauce and extra cheese. Bake at 350 degrees for 10 minutes.

*May use large can of whole tomatoes or tomato paste to thicken in place of the 2 chopped tomatoes. Serve enchiladas with sour cream and sliced black olives.*

Deb Rohovit
Iowa City, Iowa

## WALLEYE AND BACON SANDWICHES, MINNESOTA STYLE

| 6 | walleye fillets |
|---|---|
| | salt and pepper |
| | flour |
| 12 | strips bacon |
| 6 | hamburger or hot dog buns |
| | tartar sauce |

Season fillets with salt and pepper; flour lightly. Fry bacon until crisp; remove from skillet and keep warm. Pour half the fat from skillet. Fry fillets in remaining fat until golden brown. Place fried fillets on paper towel to drain. Place one warm fillet on the bottom half of a hot dog or hamburger bun. Place 2 strips of bacon on top of each fillet. Spread tartar sauce on top half of bun and enjoy. Serves 6.

*This is a favorite of all the Shive family as a shore lunch during the leisurely days of fishing from dawn to dusk. The smell of frying bacon and freshly-caught walleye cooking, mixed in with the smell of pine trees is sheer delight.*

Kay Shive
Solon, Iowa

## COLORADO BROILED TROUT

| 6 | 8-ounce dressed trout |
|---|---|
| 1/4 | cup lemon juice |
| | salt and pepper |
| 12 | strips bacon |
| | lemon wedges |
| | parsley |

Brush trout inside and out with lemon juice and sprinkle lightly with salt and pepper. Wrap 2 strips of bacon around each trout. Secure with toothpicks. Broil trout 5 inches from heat, 5 minutes per side, or until fish flakes easily when tested with a fork. Place on warm platter, garnishing with lemon wedges and sprigs of fresh parsley. Serve while warm.

Carol Brown
Solon, Iowa

# BROILED FISH WITH ARTICHOKE-CAPER SAUCE

**fish fillets (turbot, flounder, trout)**
**butter or margarine**
**salt and pepper**
**paprika (optional)**
**white wine**
**lemon juice**
**chopped artichoke hearts**
**capers**
**butter**
**white wine**
**fresh, chopped parsley**

Ingredient amounts will vary according to the number of fish fillets prepared. Wrinkle tin foil and place on broiler pan. Put small dots of butter on foil and on top of each fish fillet. Place in foiled broiler pan. Salt and pepper fish, add paprika to taste. Sprinkle each fillet with a few drops of wine and lemon juice. Broil fish until tender and moist.

*Sauce*: Chop one artichoke heart and 1/2 tablespoon capers per fillet. Place into a saucepan in which 1/2 tablespoon butter per fillet has been melted. Saute briefly. Add 1/2 tablespoon white wine and 1/2 tablespoon parsley per fillet. Mix well and remove from heat.

*To serve*: Pour sauce over hot, broiled fish. Serve with parsleyed potatoes and a mixed green salad for a low-fat low-cal meal.

*Salt can be omitted from the fish during the broiling process if you wish, as there is adequate saltiness in the sauce.*

Charles W. Markham, M.D.
Clearwater, Florida

# HONEY-FRIED FISH

| 1-1/4 | cups whole wheat flour |
|---|---|
| 1/2 | teaspoon salt |
| 1 | cup water |
| 1 | egg |
| 2 | pounds tuna, halibut, or cod steaks, cut into chunks |
| | oil for frying |
| 1 | tablespoon olive oil |
| 2 | tablespoons honey |
| 2-3 | tablespoons fresh toasted sesame seeds |

Sift flour and salt into a bowl. Make a well in the center. Combine water and egg, beat lightly, and gradually pour into the well of flour. Stir until smooth. Place 3 chunks of fish in a small bowl, pour batter over them. Set aside. Coat all pieces in this manner. Heat frying oil in a skillet or wok. Fry fish pieces a few at a time until golden. Place fried fish pieces on paper towel to drain as they are removed from hot oil. After all pieces are fried, remove cooking oil and wipe pan clean. Heat a tablespoon of fresh oil in pan, add honey, and heat mixture thoroughly. Add fish and toss to coat with honey mixture. Remove to serving plate and sprinkle with sesame seeds. Serve with plain rice.

Kay Shive
Solon, Iowa

# FRIED RAINBOW TROUT

| 6 | fresh whole rainbow trout, dressed |
|---|---|
| | salt |
| | lemon pepper |
| | flour |
| 12 | strips bacon |
| | lemon wedges |
| | parsley |

Season trout inside and out with salt and lemon pepper; flour lightly. Fry bacon, remove from skillet and keep warm. Pour excess fat from skillet. Fry trout, turning once in remaining fat in skillet until golden brown and flakes easily when tested with a fork. Place on warm platter, garnish with lemon wedges, parsley and strips of bacon. Serves 6.

Carol Brown
Solon, Iowa

# GRILLED BREAST OF WILD DUCK

Breast-out 6 wild ducks, leaving center bone; wipe each of the 6 breasts well. Rub each with salt and pepper. Slice three fresh Jalapeno peppers into thin slices, removing seeds. Slit 2, 1-inch scores, lengthwise on either sides of breast pieces. Place several thinly-sliced strips of pepper into each 1-inch slit. Be generous! Place 3 strips of bacon around breast in the opposite direction of slits. Use 2 to 3 wooden skewers for each breast to fasten bacon and close slits tightly. Grill over hot coals, 15 to 20 minutes on each side or until done to your liking. To serve, remove skewers, bacon and Jalapeno peppers. (Duck will have a slight Jalapeno flavor.)

*This recipe is awesome. It is also excellent when substituting wild dove in place of the duck. If using dove, place several breasts on one skewer. Serve either recipe with "Wild Rice". (See Vegetables and Side Dishes.)*

Michael Shive
Overland Park, Kansas

## AUNT SHIRLEY'S BARBEQUE SAUCE

| | |
|---|---|
| 10-12 | tomatoes |
| 1 | pint cold water |
| 1 | cup brown sugar |
| 1 | tablespoon salt |
| 1 | cup vinegar |
| 2 | cloves garlic, crushed |
| 2 | bay leaves |
| 1 | large onion, minced |
| 1 | tablespoon chili powder |
| 1 | teaspoon oregano, crushed |
| 1 | teaspoon black pepper |
| 2 | teaspoons dry mustard |
| | lemon juice to taste (optional) |

Simmer all ingredients over low heat for 1 hour. Stir occasionally to prevent from sticking.

*This is an easy "no-fail" recipe.*

Pamelia Eckley
Bellows Falls, Vermont

## BARBEQUE SAUCE

| | |
|---|---|
| 1 | medium-sized onion, chopped |
| 2 | tablespoons cooked meat drippings |
| 1-1/2 | cups water |
| 1 | tablespoon vinegar |
| 1 | tablespoon lemon juice |
| 1 | tablespoon Worcestershire sauce |
| 1 | cup tomato sauce |
| 2 | tablespoons liquid smoke |
| 1/2 | teaspoon salt |
| 1/4 | teaspoon paprika |
| 6 | rounded tablespoons brown sugar |

Combine all ingredients in large saucepan. Bring to boil, lower flame and simmer for 20 minutes. Pour into a jar and keep in refrigerator until needed.

Elra Currie
Bellaire Bluffs, Florida

# MUSHROOM WINE SAUCE

| | |
|---|---|
| 3 | tablespoons butter |
| 1 | pound fresh mushrooms, sliced |
| 1 | teaspoon minced onion |
| 1 | cup sherry, Madeira or Marsala wine |
| 1 | cup beef broth |
| 1/4 | teaspoon salt |
| 1/8 | teaspoon pepper |
| 1/2 | teaspoon sweet basil |
| 2 | tablespoons cornstarch |
| 2 | tablespoons water |

Melt butter in a 10-inch skillet and saute mushrooms and onions for 5 minutes. Turn off heat. Blend in wine, beef broth and seasonings and bring to a boil. Turn down heat and simmer 5 minutes. Mix cornstarch with water and add to liquid, stirring constantly. Mixture should turn clear. Makes 4 servings.

*An excellent sauce for "Prime Rib".*

Velma Weaver
Tribune, Kansas

# SAVORY SAUCE FOR LAMB

| | |
|---|---|
| 1 | medium onion |
| 2 | tablespoons butter |
| 2 | lemons, juiced |
| 1 | teaspoon mustard |
| 1 | teaspoon Worcestershire |
| 4 | beef bouillon cubes |
| 2 | cups water |
| | cornstarch dissolved in water to thicken |

Slice onion into saucepan and add next 6 ingredients. Cook over medium heat, stirring occasionally until all ingredients are dissolved and blended. Cook an additional 20 minutes. Stir in only enough cornstarch mixture to thicken to your taste. Serve very warm.

*Delicious with a "Leg of Lamb Roast" and "Brown Rice". (See Vegetables and Side Dishes.)*

Priscilla C. Hubbard
Oak Park, Illinois

## SAUCE FOR WILD FOWL

1    **6-ounce can frozen orange juice concentrate**
3/4   **cup currant jelly**
1    **teaspoon dry mustard**
1/4   **teaspoon ginger**
     **dash Tabasco sauce**

Heat all ingredients over low flame and serve warm as a compliment to wild fowl.

Barb Rathbun
Keystone, Colorado

## STEAK BASTE

1/2   **cup margarine**
1/4   **cup red wine**
1    **clove garlic, minced**
2    **teaspoons Worcestershire sauce**
1    **teaspoon minced onion**
     **dash Liquid Smoke**

Mix all ingredients together in a small saucepan and simmer over a medium hot fire on stove or grill. Makes enough sauce to baste 4 steaks.

*Baste steaks frequently and also brush on before serving.*

Velma Weaver
Tribune, Kansas

# VEGETABLES AND SIDE DISHES

Trail riders can be found throughout the resort.

# ASPARAGUS CASSEROLE

| | |
|---|---|
| 4 | tablespoons butter |
| 4 | tablespoons flour |
| 2 | cups hot milk |
| 1 | cup grated extra sharp Cheddar cheese |
| 1/4 | teaspoon salt |
| 2 | 16-ounce cans green asparagus spears |
| 4 | ounces blanched almond halves |
| 4 | tablespoons butter |
| | pepper to taste |
| 10 | crumbled saltine crackers |

Make cheese sauce by blending melted butter and flour approximately 3 minutes over low heat. Add hot milk, stirring rapidly until smooth. Add grated cheese and cook over low heat to boiling point. Add salt. Drain asparagus spears, cut into halves. Place a layer of asparagus in bottom of a 2-quart buttered casserole. Sprinkle half of almonds over asparagus. Dot with 2 tablespoons butter. Sprinkle with pepper. Add one-third of the cheese sauce. Make 2 more layers of asparagus, almonds, butter and cheese sauce. Cheese sauce will be on top. Cover with cracker crumbs and remaining butter. Bake at 350 degrees for 30 minutes. Serves 8.

*May be prepared the day before.*

Marie H. Wilson
Belleaire Bluffs, Florida

# GREEN BEAN CASSEROLE

| | |
|---|---|
| 2 | tablespoons flour |
| 3 | tablespoons melted margarine |
| 1 | teaspoon salt |
| 1/4 | teaspoon pepper |
| 1 | teaspoon sugar |
| 2 | teaspoons grated onion |
| 1 | cup sour cream |
| 2 | cans French-style green beans |
| 8 | ounces grated Cheddar cheese |
| 1/2 | cup corn flake crumbs |

Combine flour and 2 tablespoons margarine and cook gently. Remove from heat. Stir in salt, pepper, sugar, onion and sour cream. Fold in beans and put in 2-quart casserole. Cover with cheese and corn flake crumbs which have been mixed with remaining tablespoon of margarine. Bake at 350 degrees for 20 minutes. Serves 8.

Debbie Haynes
Merriam, Kansas

# SAVORY BAKED GARBANZO BEANS

| 1 | cup dry garbanzo beans |
|---|---|
| | pinch of baking soda |
| 3 | ripe tomatoes |
| 1 | large, fresh green pepper |
| 1 | onion |
| 2-5 | tablespoons olive oil |
| 2 | cloves garlic, chopped fine |
| | sweet basil |
| | tarragon |
| | parsley |
| | salt and pepper to taste |

Soak the beans in water overnight with the soda. The next day, drain and rinse the beans, and cook them in enough water to keep them covered for about 1 hour. Remove the skins from the tomatoes by dipping them for an instant into very hot water and then peeling them. Chop the tomatoes into large chunks. Slice the green pepper in matchstick pieces. Peel, quarter and thinly slice the onion. Throw the green pepper and onion slices into a pan with some hot olive oil; add also the chopped garlic, and let them saute for a few minutes. Add some crushed sweet basil, a small amount of crushed tarragon, and the chopped tomatoes. Let this mixture simmer 1 or 2 minutes while you drain the beans and remove the skins that have come loose. Finally, combine the beans with the tomato mixture, put it all into an ovenproof dish, cover tightly, and bake for 1 hour at 350 degrees. Makes 4 to 6 servings.

*Also delicious cold.*

Kay Shive
Solon, Iowa

92

## UPPER MILL TERRACE BROCCOLI CASSEROLE

2      packages chopped broccoli, cooked and drained
1      can mushroom soup
2      ounces pimento, chopped and drained
3/4    cup sour cream
1      5-ounce can sliced water chestnuts, drained
1/2    cup shredded Cheddar cheese
1      cup diced celery
       salt and pepper

Mix all ingredients and place in a 2-quart casserole. Bake 30 minutes at 350 degrees. Serves 6.

*Delicious and colorful!*

Barbara Marshall
Salina, Kansas

## BROCCOLI-RICE CASSEROLE

1-1/2  cups cooked white rice
1      10-ounce package frozen chopped broccoli, cooked and drained
1      can creamy chicken mushroom soup
1/2    8-ounce jar processed cheese spread
       salt and pepper to taste

Combine rice and broccoli with heated soup and cheese spread. Add salt and pepper to taste. Pour into a greased casserole and bake uncovered at 350 degrees about 40 minutes or until bubbling. Serves 4 generously.

Marlene Parkhurst
Greeley, Colorado

## CELERY WEDGES PARMESAN

| | |
|---|---|
| 1 | bunch celery |
| 2 | cups chicken broth |
| 2 | teaspoons chopped parsley |
| 1/4 | teaspoon oregano |
| 1/8 | teaspoon minced garlic |
| 1/2 | cup grated Parmesan cheese |
| 1/4 | cup heavy cream or half and half |
| 3 | tablespoons melted butter or margarine |
| 1/4 | teaspoon salt |
| | parsley for garnish |

Wash celery and cut off top leaves. Retain bottom but remove very bottom without separating stalks. Cut bunch lengthwise into six wedges. In a large skillet bring broth to boiling point. Mix in parsley, oregano and garlic. Add celery wedges. Cover and simmer 15 minutes or until almost tender. Drain and place in buttered 9x5x2-inch baking dish. Sprinkle with cheese. Combine cream, butter and salt; pour over celery. Bake uncovered in a preheated 325 degree oven 20 minutes or until celery is tender. Serves 6.

Charlotte Wilson Chadima
Cedar Rapids, Iowa

## ESCALLOPED CORN

| | |
|---|---|
| 1 | 16-ounce can cream-style corn |
| 1 | 16-ounce can whole corn, undrained |
| 3 | eggs, slightly beaten |
| 1 | box Jiffy corn bread mix |
| 3 | tablespoons butter or margarine |
| 1/4 | cup chopped onion |
| 1/3 | cup chopped green pepper |
| 4 | ounces Cheddar cheese, grated |

Combine first 4 ingredients. In small frying pan, saute the butter, onion and green pepper and add to corn mixture. Turn into greased casserole. Sprinkle top with cheese. Bake in a 350 degree oven for 50 minutes or until set. Serves 8.

*Very good with oysters added!*

Theresa Pagliai
West Branch, Iowa

## COLEMAN CORN PUDDING

| 2 | 16 ounce cans cream style corn |
|---|---|
| 3 | eggs, beaten |
| 2 | heaping tablespoons flour |
| 2/3 | cup sugar |
| 1 | teaspoon vanilla |
| 1 | cup evaporated milk |
| 1 | tablespoon butter |
| | dash salt |

Mix together all ingredients except butter and pour into a buttered loaf pan. Dot with the butter and bake at 350 degrees for 1-1/4 hours or until knife comes out clean when inserted in center of pudding.

Cheryl Bennett Fenderson
Davenport, Iowa

## HEAVENLY ONIONS

| 2 | large Bermuda onions, sliced and separated into rings |
|---|---|
| 2-4 | tablespoons butter |
| 1/2 | pound Swiss cheese, grated |
| 1/4 | teaspoon pepper |
| 1/2 | cup milk |
| 1 | teaspoon soy sauce |
| 1 | can cream of chicken soup |
| 8 | slices French bread, buttered on both sides |

Simmer onions in butter in heavy pan on low heat until tender, stirring constantly. Put in 1-quart casserole. Top with cheese and pepper. Heat milk, soy sauce and soup; stir until blended. Pour soup mixture over all. Stir gently with a knife to mix well. Overlap bread slices in a ring on top of onion mixture. Bake for 30 minutes at 350 degrees. Serves 4 to 6.

Mrs. Ivan Auer
Naperville, Illinois

## PUREE OF PARSNIPS

| | |
|---|---|
| 1 | cup heavy cream |
| 1 | cup sour cream |
| 1-1/2 | pounds parsnips |
| 2-3 | carrots |
| 1/4 | cup water |
| 5 | tablespoons creme fraiche (recipe below) |
| | salt and pepper to taste |

*Creme Fraiche:* Whisk together heavy cream and sour cream; cover loosely and let set in warm spot overnight or until thickened. Refrigerate 4 hours or for up to 2 weeks.

*Puree:* Trim and peel parsnips and carrots; chop into 1/3-inch slices. Place in a 1-1/2- quart casserole with 1/4 cup water. Microwave on full power 10 to 15 minutes, stirring once. When parsnips are tender, place vegetables in food processor and process. Place in top of double boiler the creme fraiche, seasonings and vegetable puree. Steam for 20 to 30 minutes on low heat. Allow casserole to stand a few minutes before serving. Serves 4 to 6.

Mary Lou Hattery
Cedar Rapids, Iowa

## HASH BROWNS

| | |
|---|---|
| 2 | pounds frozen hashed brown potatoes |
| 1/2 | cup melted butter |
| 1 | can cream of chicken soup |
| 1 | can Cheddar cheese soup |
| 1/2 | chopped onion |
| 1 | pint sour cream |
| | salt and pepper to taste |
| 2 | cups crushed corn flakes |
| 1/4 | cup butter |

Combine potatoes, butter, soups, onion, sour cream, salt and pepper. Pour into a 2-quart casserole. Top with the crushed corn flakes mixed with 1/4 cup butter. Bake at 350 degrees for 1 hour. Serves 6 to 8.

Dorris Davis
Webster Groves, Missouri

## POTATOES ROMANOFF

5     cups diced, cooked potatoes (about 6 baking potatoes)
2     teaspoons salt
2     cups creamed cottage cheese
1     cup sour cream
1/4  cup finely minced green onion
1     small clove garlic, crushed
      grated Cheddar cheese
      paprika

Cook unpeeled potatoes only until tender, then cool, peel and cut into cubes. Sprinkle with 1 teaspoon salt. Combine cottage cheese, sour cream, onion and garlic with remaining salt. Fold in potatoes and put into a buttered 1-1/2-quart casserole. Top with as much grated Cheddar cheese as you care to use and sprinkle lightly with paprika. Bake in a 350 degree oven for 40 to 45 minutes or until thoroughly heated and cheese has melted. Serves 10.

Wilma Sykes
Englewood, Colorado

## PAT'S POTATOES

7     pieces bacon
8     red potatoes
2     cups grated Cheddar cheese
4     tablespoons melted butter

Crisply fry bacon and drain. Peel raw potatoes and slice. Lay in bottom of casserole. Crumble bacon on top. Cover with Cheddar cheese. Pour melted butter over all. Bake covered, 45 minutes at 350 degrees. Uncover and continue to bake 15 minutes to brown.

Priscilla C. Hubbard
Oak Park, Illinois

# BROWN RICE

1      cup uncooked regular rice
2      cans beef consomme
1      tablespoon onion flakes
1/4    cup butter

Combine all ingredients in casserole. Cover and bake for 1 hour at 350 degrees. Serves 6.

*Serve with "Mrs. Kmet's Chicken". (See Entrees.)*

Priscilla C. Hubbard
Oak Park, Illinois

# OVEN RICE

1      cup long-grain rice
2-1/4  cups water
1      teaspoon salt

Mix together and place in 1-1/2-quart casserole dish. Cover and bake 1 hour in a 350 degree oven. Fluff with fork half way through baking.

Katy Ahmann
Los Altos, California

# WILD RICE

| | |
|---|---|
| 1 | cup wild rice |
| 3 | cups water |
| 4 | tablespoons butter |
| 1 | teaspoon salt |
| 1 | 4-ounce can mushrooms |

Clean wild rice by washing many times. Remove small pieces of chaff. Drain. Place rice in pan and add water, butter, salt, mushrooms and mushroom liquid. Cook, covered, until rice is tender, stirring several times, about 45 minutes. You can use canned chicken broth or canned beef broth instead of water. Omit salt if either is used.

*Good served with "Wild Breast of Duck". (See Entrees.)*

Michael Shive
Overland Park, Kansas

# KAPUSTA (SWEET POLISH SAUERKRAUT)

| | |
|---|---|
| 1 | quart jar sauerkraut |
| 2 | beef bouillon cubes |
| 1 | cup hot water |
| 1/4 | cup brown sugar |
| 4 | slices raw bacon, chopped |
| 1 | medium onion, chopped fine |
| 3 | tablespoons flour |

Rinse sauerkraut thoroughly to remove all brine. Press gently between paper toweling. Dissolve bouillon cubes in water. Put well-drained sauerkraut into saucepan. Add the bouillon and brown sugar and toss lightly. Boil 20 to 30 minutes. When sauerkraut is done, drain, reserving juices.

Meanwhile, cook bacon until crisp; remove to drain and reserve drippings. Add onion to pan and cook until lightly browned. Add flour, stirring until browned. Add reserved sauerkraut juices to bacon/onion/flour mixture. Cook, stirring constantly, until smooth and slightly thickened. Add drained sauerkraut and toss lightly.

*This yummy recipe is from my mother in Caseville, Michigan.*

Pat Hubbard
Keystone, Colorado

# TOMATO PIE

| 1 | pie crust, partially baked |
| 2-3 | large tomatoes, sliced |
| | pinch sweet basil |
| 1 | small bunch green onions, cleaned and chopped |
| | salt and pepper |
| 3/4 | cup mayonnaise |
| 1-1/2 | cups grated sharp Cheddar cheese |

Crust should be almost done but not brown. Place tomato slices in crust and sprinkle basil, onions, salt and pepper on top. Mix mayonnaise and cheese and spread over tomatoes. Bake in a 400 degree oven 20 to 25 minutes.

*Nice for brunch or as a vegetable accompaniment to meat.*

Rene Pagliai
Iowa City, Iowa


# SPINACH/NOODLE CASSEROLE

| 1 | 10-ounce box spinach, thawed, drained |
| 1/2 | can mushroom soup |
| 6 | ounces sour cream |
| 1/2 | tablespoon minced onion |
| | salt and pepper to taste |
| 6-8 | ounces cooked flat noodles |
| 8 | ounces processed cheese spread |

Combine spinach, soup, sour cream, onion, salt and pepper. Place half of the noodles in a greased, 1-1/2-quart casserole, then half of the spinach mixture. Top with 4 ounces of the cheese spread. Repeat layers, topping with remaining cheese spread. Bake at 350 degrees for 1 hour. Serves 6 to 8.

Dorris Davis
Webster Groves, Missouri

# SOUTHERN ZUCCHINI CASSEROLE

8-10    medium zucchini
        water to cover zucchini
        salt to taste
1       cup minced onion
4       tablespoons butter
2       eggs
1-1/2  cups grated Cheddar cheese
        bread crumbs

Wash zucchini and slice into rounds about 1/4-inch thick. Cover with water; salt lightly and boil 8 to 10 minutes until barely tender. Drain zucchini and cut slices in half. Fry onions in butter over medium heat until tender but not brown; remove from heat. Beat 2 eggs and add zucchini. Combine this mixture with the butter and onion, blend well and bring to a boil over medium heat, stirring constantly. Remove from heat, add grated cheese and mix well. Taste and add salt as needed. Spoon into a buttered 9x13-inch casserole and top with bread crumbs. Bake at 350 degrees for 25 to 30 minutes until bubbling hot. Serves 8 to 10.

*Can be prepared ahead and kept refrigerated 1 day before baking.*

Nena Graden
Akron, Ohio

# CHEEZY VEGETABLE CASSEROLE

2       16-ounce bags frozen vegetables (carrots, cauliflower, broccoli combination)
1       can cream of mushroom soup
1       8-ounce jar processed cheese spread
1       can mushrooms (optional)
1       can onion rings

Partially cook vegetables until tender crisp. Drain thoroughly. Heat soup and cheese spread in saucepan, mixing well. Add mushrooms. Place vegetables into a buttered 9x9-inch casserole. Pour soup mixture over vegetables. Bake at 350 degrees for 30 minutes, adding onion rings to top of dish during last 10 minutes of baking. Serves 8.

*Any vegetable combination could be used. For a larger group use one additional package of vegetables plus an additional one-half jar of processed cheese spread and one-half can of soup. Can be prepared early in day and baked later.*

Donna Bray
West Des Moines, Iowa

# RUSSIAN VEGETABLE PIE

| 1-1/4 | cups flour |
| 1 | teaspoon sugar |
| 1 | teaspoon salt |
| 4 | ounces softened cream cheese |
| 3 | tablespoons butter |
| 1 | small head cabbage, shredded (about 3 cups) |
| 1/2 | pound mushrooms |
| 1 | yellow onion |
| 3 | tablespoons butter |
| 1/8 | teaspoon basil |
| 1/8 | teaspoon marjoram |
| 1/8 | teaspoon tarragon |
| | salt and fresh ground pepper, to taste |
| 4 | ounces cream cheese, softened |
| 4-5 | hard-cooked eggs |
| 1/8 | teaspoon chopped dill |

Make a pastry by sifting together the flour, sugar and salt. Cut in the cream cheese and butter and work together. Roll out two-thirds of the pastry and line a 9-inch pie dish. Roll out remaining pastry and make a circle large enough to cover the dish. Put into refrigerator to chill.

Shred the cabbage coarsely. Wash the mushrooms and slice. Peel and chop the onion. In a large skillet, melt 2 tablespoons butter. Add the onion and cabbage and saute for several

minutes, stirring constantly. Add at least 1/8 teaspoon each of basil, marjoram, and tarragon (all crushed), and some salt and fresh-ground pepper. Stirring often, allow the mixture to cook until the cabbage is wilted and the onions soft. Remove from the pan and set aside.

Add another tablespoon of butter to the pan and saute the mushrooms lightly for about 5 or 6 minutes, stirring constantly. Spread the softened cream cheese in the bottom of the pie shell. Slice the eggs and arrange the slices in a layer over the cheese. Sprinkle them with a little chopped dill, then cover them with the cabbage. Make a final layer with the sauteed mushrooms and cover with the chilled circle of pastry.

Press the pastry together lightly at the edges, and flute with a sharp knife; cut a few short slashes through the top crust. Bake in a 400 degree oven for 15 minutes, then turn the temperature down to 350 degrees and continue baking for another 20 to 25 minutes, or until the crust is light brown. Serves 4 to 6.

*This is great thinly sliced for snacking, but is very rich and may be used as a main dish.*

Kay Shive
Solon, Iowa

# SALADS AND SALAD DRESSINGS

The rustic elegance of the Keystone Ranch welcomes dinner guests summer and winter.

# BROCCOLI SALAD

1      bottle Italian dressing
1      package Italian dressing seasoning
3/4   cup green olives
1      can water chestnuts
2      bunches fresh broccoli, cut up
1      cup sliced celery
2      tomatoes, chopped
2      onions, sliced

Make a marinade by combining Italian dressing and seasoning. Place olives, chestnuts, broccoli and celery into dressing and set into refrigerator to marinate at least 4 hours. Before serving, add the tomatoes and onions.

*This recipe may vary with whatever you have in your cupboard or refrigerator. For instance, if you don't have celery, substitute another crispy vegetable such as carrots; or cauliflower for broccoli. Black olives can replace the green olives, and water chestnuts can be replaced with slivered almonds.*

Kay Shive
Solon, Iowa

# AUNT PAULINE'S SALAD

garden lettuce
chives
salt
pepper
sugar
vinegar
buttermilk

Tear up lettuce into small pieces. Add chives, salt, pepper, sugar and vinegar. Refrigerate 15 minutes. Pour buttermilk over salad. Taste and add more of whatever ingredient pleases your taste buds. Serve with a meal of meat and mashed potatoes.

*This is a recipe from "The Old School of Cooking". Nothing is measured—it's made according to your own individual taste. That is—add and taste, add and taste!*

Jody Laschanzky
Littleton, Colorado

# LAYER SALAD

| 1/2 | head lettuce |
| 1 | cup chopped celery |
| 1 | cup grated carrots |
| 1 | cup chopped cauliflower |
| 1 | cup chopped broccoli |
| 1 | cup mushrooms |
| 1 | cup peas |
| 1 | pound bacon, fried until crisp and crumbled |
| 5 | eggs, hard-cooked, sliced |
| 1-1/2 | cups mayonnaise |
| 3 | tablespoons milk |
| 2 | tablespoons vinegar or lemon juice |
| 1-1/2 | cups grated Cheddar cheese |

Tear lettuce and place as bottom layer in a 9x12-inch glass dish. Then, in layers, place celery, carrots, cauliflower, broccoli, mushrooms, peas and bacon. Over the bacon, arrange the slices of hard-cooked eggs.

In a separate bowl, mix together the mayonnaise, milk and vinegar. Spread over vegetables and cover with the grated cheese. Seal salad with foil and place in refrigerator overnight.

Anna Vicelli
Dillon, Colorado

# FRESH TARRAGON SPINACH SALAD

| 1/2 | cup salad oil |
| 2 | tablespoons wine vinegar |
| 1 | teaspoon sugar |
| 1/2 | teaspoon salt |
| 1/2 | teaspoon dried tarragon, crumbled |
| 1/4 | teaspoon coarsely ground black pepper |
| 1 | bunch spinach leaves, stems removed, rinsed well and drained |
| 2 | eggs, hard-cooked and pressed through sieve |
| 6 | slices bacon, cooked very crisp and crumbled |

Shake together in a jar the first 6 ingredients. Set aside. Place spinach leaves in a chilled salad bowl. Toss with tarragon dressing to coat well. Sprinkle with eggs and top with bacon.

Kay Shive
Solon, Iowa

# CAULIFLOWER SALAD

1-1/2  teaspoons dry Original Hidden Valley Ranch dressing
1      cup mayonnaise
1/4    cup milk
1      head fresh cauliflower, broken up
1      cup chopped celery
1/2    cup chopped onion
1      10-ounce package frozen peas
1      cup sliced radishes

Shake together first 3 ingredients and pour over prepared vegetables. Let stand overnight in refrigerator. Serves 8 to 10.

Betty Oglesby
Iowa City, Iowa

# CURRIED TOMATO SALAD

6      large tomatoes, peeled and cut into bite-sized pieces
1      small white onion, finely chopped
1      teaspoon salt
1/4    teaspoon coarsely ground black pepper
2      tablespoons minced fresh parsley
1/2    cup mayonnaise
1      teaspoon curry powder

Combine tomatoes, onion, salt, pepper, and parsley in a bowl; cover and refrigerate for 3 hours. Combine mayonnaise and curry in a bowl; cover and chill for 3 hours. To serve, spoon tomato mixture into small bowls; top each with a spoonful of mayonnaise mixture. Makes 8 servings.

Kay Shive
Solon, Iowa

## FIVE-LAYER SALAD

| 1 | head cauliflower, broken into small pieces |
| 1 | small head crisp lettuce, torn into small pieces |
| 1 | large Bermuda onion, cut into very thin slices |
| 1 | pound bacon, cooked very crisp and crumbled |
| 1/4 | cup sugar |
| 1 | cup mayonnaise |
| 1/3 | cup sour cream |
| 2 | tomatoes, chopped |

In bottom of large glass salad bowl layer salad as follows: Cauliflower, lettuce, onion and bacon. Combine sugar, mayonnaise and sour cream and spread on top. Place into refrigerator overnight. Add tomatoes just before serving. To serve, toss lightly or scoop with large spoon from bottom of bowl.

*If making this the day you will serve it, cool several hours.*

Pat Hubbard
Keystone, Colorado


## B.L.T. SALAD

| 8 | slices bacon |
| 1 | small head lettuce |
| 4 | medium tomatoes |
| | salt (optional) |
| | pepper |
| 1/4 | cup Miracle Whip salad dressing |
| 2 | tablespoons milk |

Fry bacon until crisp and drain on paper toweling. Break each slice of bacon into 3 or 4 pieces. In salad bowl, tear lettuce into bite-sized pieces. Cut tomatoes into wedges and arrange over lettuce. Sprinkle with salt and pepper. Arrange bacon on tomatoes and refrigerate salad until needed. In small container, combine salad dressing with milk and refrigerate. Toss salad at the table and serve with dressing.

Mary Feehan
Iowa City, Iowa

# JOE'S WORLD FAMOUS TABOULI

| | |
|---|---|
| 1 | cucumber |
| 1/2 | bunch scallions |
| 1 | green pepper |
| 2 | 8-ounce cans mushrooms |
| 1 | 12-ounce can black olives |
| 2 | whole tomatoes |
| 2 | cups bulgur wheat |
| 1/2 | cup lemon juice |
| 1/2 | cup olive oil |

Chop all vegetables into small pieces. Combine vegetables and bulgur wheat in a bowl. Thoroughly combine lemon juice and olive oil in a separate cup. Add to vegetables and wheat. Mix well and let stand in refrigerator overnight (or at least 8 hours). Serves 6. Add any ingredients you wish such as parsley, beans, alfalfa sprouts or water chestnuts.

*This salad provides a good supply of carbohydrates and has low fat content for skiing energy!*

Keystone Village Ski Rental
Keystone Resort

# OAK PARK POTATO SALAD

| | |
|---|---|
| 7 | medium potatoes, cooked, cooled and cubed |
| 7 | pieces bacon |
| 4 | green onions, diced |
| 3 | stalks celery, diced |
| 1 | green pepper, diced |
| 3 | tablespoons mayonnaise |
| | salt and pepper |
| 1 | egg, hard boiled |
| | paprika |

Boil potatoes and cool. Crisply fry the bacon, drain on paper towel and reserve 3 tablespoons drippings. Into a medium bowl, combine potatoes, crumbled bacon, onions, celery and green pepper. In separate small bowl, combine the reserved bacon drippings, mayonnaise, and salt and pepper to taste. Toss into potato mixture. Garnish with sliced hard-boiled egg and sprinkle lightly with paprika.

Priscilla C. Hubbard
Oak Park, Illinois

# CHILI TACO SALAD

| | |
|---|---|
| 1 | pound ground beef |
| 1/3 | cup chopped onion |
| 1 | envelope taco seasoning |
| 1 | 16-ounce can stewed tomatoes |
| 1 | 15-ounce can drained kidney beans |
| 1/2 | cup water |
| | chili powder to taste |
| | lettuce leaves |
| | taco flavored corn chips |
| | shredded lettuce |
| | shredded Monterey Jack cheese |
| | chopped avocado |
| | chopped tomatoes |
| | sour cream |

Brown the ground beef with the onion, pour off excess fat. Stir in taco seasoning, stewed tomatoes, kidney beans, water and chili powder. Simmer one hour, stirring occasionally until thickened. To serve, cover each plate with large lettuce leaves. Add a generous handful of chips and top with the chili. Garnish with shredded lettuce, cheese, avocado, tomatoes and sour cream.

Marlene Parkhurst
Greeley, Colorado

# CHICKEN LIVER SALAD

| | |
|---|---|
| 1/2 | pound chicken livers |
| | butter |
| 1 | tablespoon instant minced onion |
| 1/16 | teaspoon garlic powder |
| 1 | tablespoon water |
| 6-8 | canned water chestnuts |
| 2 | tablespoons fresh lime or lemon juice |
| 1/4 | cup salad oil |
| 1 | teaspoon soy or Tamari sauce |
| 1 | teaspoon brown sugar |
| 1 | tablespoon finely chopped candied ginger |
| 1 | quart chilled salad greens |

Cook chicken livers gently in a little butter until tender. Set aside and cool. Stir onion and garlic powder into water. Cut chestnuts into thin slices and add to onion and garlic. Combine lime juice, oil, soy sauce, sugar and ginger. Mix all ingredients and toss gently. Serve on chilled salad plate lined with lettuce.

Annabelle Gunther Meyer
Pewaukee, Wisconsin

# CRANBERRY COMPOTE

1     medium orange
1     12-ounce package fresh cranberries
1-1/2 cups sugar
1     cup golden raisins
1     teaspoon salt
1/4  teaspoon allspice
1/4  teaspoon cinnamon
1     16-ounce can sliced peaches, drained
1     16-ounce can sliced pears, drained
1     16-ounce can apricot halves, drained

From the orange, grate 1 teaspoon orange peel and squeeze enough juice to make 1/4 cup. In saucepan over high heat, mix orange peel, orange juice and next 6 ingredients. Stir until boiling, then cover and simmer until cranberries pop and liquid is thickened. Add peaches, pears and apricots and heat thoroughly. Serve warm or cover and chill to serve at a later time.

*Remember to stir cranberry mixture frequently so that cranberries don't burn.*

Cynthia Hubbard Shive
Iowa City, Iowa

# CRANBERRY SALAD

1     pound fresh cranberries, ground
1     20-ounce can crushed pineapple, well drained
1     pound miniature marshmallows
1     cup heavy cream, whipped to stiff peaks
3/4  cup sugar
      apples, chopped (optional)
      nuts, chopped (optional)

Mix all ingredients together and pour into a 9x13-inch pan or attractive glass serving bowl. Refrigerate until serving.

*Can substitute 1 envelope Dream Whip following package directions but omitting sugar, or...you can use 2 cups prepared whipped topping.*

Lorraine M. Lee
Lakewood, Colorado

## TANGY CRAN-RASPBERRY HOLIDAY MOLD

| 1 | 3-ounce package lemon gelatin |
| 1 | 3-ounce package raspberry gelatin |
| 1-1/2 | cups boiling water |
| 1 | can jellied cran-raspberry sauce |
| 1 | 10-ounce package frozen raspberries, thawed and undrained |
| 1 | 7-ounce bottle 7-Up |
| 1/4 | cup chopped pecans |

Dissolve packages of gelatin in boiling water. Add cran-raspberry sauce which has been broken up into pieces. Add thawed raspberries and chill 25 to 30 minutes until partially set. Gently fold in 7-Up and pecans and pour into a greased 9-cup mold. Chill until set and firm. Unmold and serve on leafy green lettuce. Serves 8.

Terry Biddinger
Littleton, Colorado

## FIX 'N' SKI SALAD

| 1 | can apricot or peach pie filling |
| 1 | 9-ounce container prepared whipped topping |
| 1 | #2 can crushed pineapple, undrained |
| 1 | can sweetened condensed milk |
| | chopped nuts (optional) |

Combine first 4 ingredients. Pour into 9x13-inch pan or individual paper cupcake cups. Sprinkle top with nuts if desired. Place in freezer. Remove 20 minutes before serving. Serves 8 to 10.

Betty Oglesby
Iowa City, Iowa

## BLUEBERRY-CREAM GELATIN SALAD

| | |
|---|---|
| 1 | cup cream |
| 2/3 | cup sugar |
| 1 | envelope unflavored gelatin |
| 1/4 | cup cold water |
| 1/2 | pint sour cream |
| 1 | teaspoon vanilla |
| 1 | package raspberry gelatin |
| 1 | cup boiling water |
| 1 | 14-1/2 ounce can blueberries with juice |

In saucepan, heat cream and sugar but do not boil. Stir in gelatin which has been dissolved in the cold water. Cool slightly and blend in sour cream and vanilla. Pour into a 9x9x2-inch pan. Refrigerate for 1 hour.

Dissolve the raspberry gelatin in 1 cup boiling water. Add blueberries with juice. Cool and pour carefully over soft-set first layer. Refrigerate until firm. Serves 12.

*This is one of my family's favorites!*

Betty Oglesby
Iowa City, Iowa

## PEACHES AND CREAM GELATIN SALAD

| | |
|---|---|
| 1 | large can sliced cling peaches |
| 2 | 3-ounce packages peach-flavored gelatin |
| 1-1/2 | cups hot water |
| 1 | 8-ounce package cream cheese, softened |
| 1 | cup whipped topping |

Drain peaches, reserving juice. Dissolve gelatin in hot water. Measure peach juice and add enough water to make 1-1/2 cups. Stir into gelatin and refrigerate until consistency of syrup. Place cream cheese in mixing bowl and beat until smooth. Add drained peaches and beat again. Add chilled gelatin to cream cheese and peaches. Beat until fluffy. Fold in whipped topping. Pour into salad mold or 9x13-inch pan and chill until firm.

Mary Feehan
Iowa City, Iowa

## EASY SALAD

| | |
|---|---|
| 1 | 15-ounce can crushed pineapple, slightly drained |
| 1 | 14-ounce can sweetened condensed milk |
| 1 | 9-ounce container prepared whipped topping |
| 1 | can cherry pie filling |
| 2 | tablespoons lemon juice |

Combine all ingredients and pour into 9x13-inch glass dish. Refrigerate over night.

Corinne Jacobson
Rockford, Illinois

## CAROL BROWN'S HERB DRESSING

| | |
|---|---|
| 1/3 | cup white vinegar |
| 2/3 | cup vegetable oil |
| 1 | teaspoon sugar |
| 1 | teaspoon crushed basil leaves or salad herbs |
| 1/4 | teaspoon paprika |
| 1/8 | teaspoon salt (optional) |

Mix in glass measuring cup until dissolved. Pour into tightly-sealed bottle and refrigerate.

Carol Brown
Solon, Iowa

# MAD RIVER VALLEY FRENCH DRESSING

1/2     cup ketchup
1/2     cup salad oil
1/4     cup cider vinegar
2       teaspoons confectioners' sugar
1       clove garlic, split
1/4     teaspoon salt
        dash pepper

Combine all ingredients in a tightly-sealed jar and shake vigorously. Chill to blend flavors. Remove garlic and shake again
before serving. Makes 1-1/4 cups dressing.

*I discovered this recipe in Mad River Valley, Vermont—easy,
delicious and keeps well.*

Pat Hubbard
Keystone, Colorado

Keystone Minor's Camp

DESSERTS

# PRESERVED CHILDREN

| | |
|---|---|
| 1 | large mountainside |
| 1/2 | dozen children |
| 1/2 | dozen pairs of skis |
| 1 | good ski instructor |
| 1 | large bunch of snow |
| | unlimited clear mountain air and sunshine |

Mix the children, skis and instructor well together. Sprinkle the mountainside with snow and spread with people mixture. Cover with clear air and bake in the sunshine. When done, keep warm by crackling fire until ready to tuck into bed.

# SHREDDED NEWSPAPER CAKE (OR... POPPY SEED CAKE)

| | |
|---|---|
| 2/3 | cup milk |
| 1/3 | cup poppy seeds |
| 2-1/2 | cups flour |
| 3/4 | tablespoon baking powder |
| 1/4 | teaspoon salt |
| 1-1/2 | cups sugar |
| 1/2 | cup butter, softened |
| 2 | teaspoons vanilla extract |
| 1/2 | cup milk |
| 4 | large egg whites |
| 1/4 | cup sugar |
| 8 | ounces cream cheese, softened |
| 1/3 | cup butter, softened |
| 2-1/2 | cups confectioners' sugar |
| 1/2 | teaspoon lemon juice, fresh |

In a saucepan, bring 2/3 cup milk to a boil and add poppy seeds; set aside to cool. Sift together flour, baking powder and salt; set aside. Cream 1-1/2 cups sugar and 1/2 cup softened butter until creamy. Add vanilla extract; set aside.

Add 1/2 cup milk to the poppy seed mixture. In separate bowl, beat egg whites until soft peaks form. Slowly add the 1/4 cup sugar and beat until soft peaks form again. Mix poppy seed mixture into the creamed sugar and butter mixture, alternating with the dry ingredients. Fold into the egg whites.

Pour batter into 2, greased and floured, 8-inch round pans and bake in a preheated 375 degree oven for 30 minutes.

*Frosting*: Beat together until creamy the cream cheese and remaining ingredients.

*This cake is so good, it's now our traditional family birthday cake.*

Chuck Brown
Keystone Resort

119

# CHOCOLATE MINT BROWNIES

| | |
|---|---|
| 2 | 1-ounce squares unsweetened chocolate |
| 1/2 | cup butter |
| 1 | cup sugar |
| 2 | eggs, beaten |
| 1 | teaspoon vanilla |
| 1 | cup flour |
| 1/2 | cup chopped walnuts |
| 2 | cups powdered sugar |
| 4 | tablespoons butter, softened |
| 2 | tablespoons half and half |
| 2 | tablespoons peppermint extract |
| | green food coloring as desired |
| 2 | 1-ounce squares unsweetened chocolate |
| 2 | tablespoons butter |

*Brownies:* Melt 2 ounces of chocolate and butter together and cool. Mix with 1 cup sugar, 2 eggs, vanilla, flour and walnuts. Spoon into greased 12x8-inch pan and bake at 350 degrees for 20 minutes. Check at 15 minutes with toothpick. Remove when just a few crumbs stick. Over baking will cause dryness. Cool thoroughly.

*Mint Layer:* Beat well the powdered sugar, 4 tablespoons butter, half and half, peppermint extract and the food coloring, if you desire to include it. Spread over cooled brownies. Let stand until set.

*Chocolate Frosting:* Melt remaining unsweetened chocolate and butter. Cool. Drizzle and lightly spread over mint layer. Let set about 1 hour; cut into squares or rectangles, leave in pan and cover with foil, refrigerating until ready to serve. Serves 12.

Marlene Parkhurst
Greeley, Colorado

# DANISH CHEESECAKE

3-1/2   cups finely crushed graham cracker crumbs
2       teaspoons cinnamon
1       cup melted butter
3       eggs, well-beaten
2       8-ounce packages cream cheese, softened
1       cup sugar
1/4     teaspoon salt
2       teaspoons vanilla extract
1/2     teaspoon almond extract
3       cups sour cream

*Crust*: Combine the first three ingredients, saving out 3 tablespoons for garnish. Press the remainder into the bottom and sides of a 9-inch spring-form pan.

*Filling*: In bowl, combine eggs, cream cheese, sugar, salt and extracts and beat until smooth. Blend in sour cream. Pour into graham cracker crust and sprinkle with reserved crumbs. Bake in a 375 degree oven for 30 minutes or until just set. It will wobble in the middle like gelatin. Chill well—4 to 5 hours in the refrigerator. Overnight is best.

*This is an authentic Danish cheesecake.*

Kirsten Price
Keystone, Colorado

# CHRISTMAS CRANBERRY DESSERT

2       cups cranberries
2       cups unpeeled, chopped apples
1/2     cup sugar
1/2     cup walnuts
2       eggs
1       cup sugar
1       cup flour
1/2     cup melted butter
1/2     cup melted shortening

Place cranberries and apples in an oiled 10-inch pie plate and sprinkle with the 1/2 cup sugar and the nuts. Beat eggs, add sugar and cream thoroughly. Add flour, melted butter, and shortening and beat well. Pour over fruit. Bake at 325 degrees for 60 minutes or until crust is golden.

*Serve warm or cold with cream poured over top or with ice cream. This dessert freezes nicely.*

Sunny McNall
Cedar Rapids, Iowa

# CREAM PUFFS

| 1/2 | cup butter |
| 1 | cup boiling water |
| 1 | cup flour |
| 1/4 | teaspoon salt |
| 4 | eggs |
| 2 | cups milk |
| 2 | eggs |
| 1/4 | cup sugar |
| 2 | tablespoons butter |
| 1 | teaspoon vanilla |

*Puffs:* Over low heat, melt 1/2 cup butter in the boiling water. Add flour and salt all at once, stirring vigorously. Cook and stir until mixture forms ball and doesn't separate. Cool to just warm and add eggs, 1 at a time, beating until smooth. Drop by tablespoons 3 inches apart on a greased cookie sheet. Bake in a preheated 450 degree oven for 15 minutes and then at 325 degrees for 25 minutes. Remove from oven and split partially. Turn oven off and put puffs back into dry for about 20 minutes. Cool on a rack. Makes 10 puffs.

*Filling:* In medium saucepan, cook milk on low flame. When warm add all but vanilla, stirring constantly until thick. Add vanilla. After pudding cools and before spooning into puffs, beat with mixer until nice and smooth. Fill puffs when ready to serve.

*I think these are fun to make.*

Dorothy Bennett
Iowa City, Iowa

# PECAN TORTE

12    eggs, separated
2     cups sugar
      pinch of salt
1     cup crushed soda crackers
1     cup broken pecans
3/4   teaspoon vanilla
2     cups brown sugar
1     pint heavy cream
1/2   cup butter

Separate eggs. Beat yokes, sugar and salt until thickened to the consistency of custard. In another large bowl beat whites until stiff but not dry. Fold about half cup of the beaten egg whites into yolk mixture, then fold all yolk mixture into whites. Gently fold in crushed soda crackers, pecans and vanilla.

Pour into well-greased (sides and bottom) 9x13-inch pan. Bake in a preheated 375 degree oven for 30 minutes. Allow to cool at room temperature. Torte will fall after removing from oven.

*Caramel Sauce:* Mix brown sugar, cream and butter and boil gently for five minutes, stirring constantly.

*To Serve:* Cut torte into squares, spoon caramel sauce on top and garnish with a spoonful of whipped cream. Serves 16.

*Torte must be stored in the refrigerator. Keeps 3 to 4 days.*

Bettie Hunchis
Edina, Minnesota

## OPEN FACED APPLE PIE

| | |
|---|---|
| 1 | 9-inch pie crust |
| 1 | 5-pound bag tart apples (Do not use Granny Smith apples—Jonathans are best.) |
| | sugar |
| 1 | cup heavy cream |
| 3/4 | cup sugar |
| | cinnamon |
| | butter |

Preheat oven to 450 degrees. Begin to fill crust with peeled, cored and sliced apples. When crust is half filled, sprinkle some sugar over the apples. Continue adding apples until heaping. Combine the cream and 1/2- to 3/4-cup sugar—according to your taste and the tartness of the apples. Pour over apples. Top with cinnamon and sugar and dot with butter. Place in oven. After 15 minutes, reduce heat to 350 degrees and cover with lid or foil to protect crust from burning, and bake for 30 minutes. Test apples until done with toothpick. Remove foil and bake an additional 15 minutes to brown.

*This wonderful pie is an original from my grandmother, Lillie Jagim, of Van Horne, Iowa.*

Cheryl Bennett Fenderson
Davenport, Iowa

## PECAN PIE

| | |
|---|---|
| 1 | cup corn syrup |
| 3 | eggs, lightly beaten |
| | pinch salt |
| 1 | teaspoon vanilla |
| 1 | cup sugar |
| 2 | tablespoons butter, melted |
| 1 | cup pecan pieces or halves |
| 1 | unbaked 9-inch pie shell |

Combine all ingredients. Pour into pie shell. Bake 15 minutes at 400 degrees. Reduce heat to 350 degrees. Bake 30 minutes more. Makes 8 servings.

Variation for high altitudes: Try original recipe first, then experiment if necessary with 1 additional egg and baking 1 hour at 350 degrees.

*I created this recipe for the University of Texas cookbook, Cook 'em Horns.*

Nancy Wilson
Dallas, Texas

# PEAR PIE

| | |
|---|---|
| 1 | cup flour |
| 1/2 | teaspoon salt |
| 1/3 | cup lard or shortening |
| 2 | tablespoons cold water |
| 7 | firm, medium-sized pears |
| 1/2 | cup sugar |
| 1/4 | teaspoon cinnamon |
| 2 | tablespoons tapioca |
| 1/4 | teaspoon almond extract |
| 1/2 | cup butter |
| 1/3 | cup chopped almonds |
| 1 | cup flour |
| 1/2 | cup brown sugar |
| 1/2 | teaspoon cinnamon |

In a bowl, cut together flour, salt and lard. Add cold water a few drops at a time until dough forms into a ball without crumbling. Work dough as little as possible to keep from getting tough. Roll out on a floured baking board and place into greased and floured pie pan, crimping edges.

Preheat oven to 400 degrees. Peel and slice pears. Place in a medium-sized saucepan, add next 4 ingredients and stir lightly. Let stand 5 minutes and then pour into pastry-lined pan. Mix remaining ingredients until crumbly and sprinkle over pie. Bake 25 to 30 minutes.

*This pie was my first and only entry in the Iowa State Fair where it received many favorable reviews.*

Judy Miller
Solon, Iowa

# CHOCOLATE ECLAIR CAKE

| 1 | box graham crackers |
| 2 | 3-ounce packages vanilla instant pudding |
| 3 | cups milk |
| 8 | ounces prepared whipped topping |
| 2 | 1-ounce packages Nestlés liquid chocolate |
| 2 | teaspoons light corn syrup |
| 2 | teaspoons vanilla |
| 1-1/2 | cups confectioners' sugar |
| 3 | tablespoons melted butter |
| 3 | tablespoons milk |

Line a 9x13-inch pan with one-third of the graham crackers. Mix pudding and milk until it thickens; then fold whipped topping into pudding mixture. Pour half of pudding mixture over graham crackers. Cover pudding layer with another graham cracker layer, followed by the rest of the pudding and then the graham crackers. Refrigerate for 2 hours while you make the topping.

*Topping:* Mix the liquid chocolate, corn syrup, vanilla, sugar, melted butter and milk all together until blended well. Pour over chilled graham crackers and pudding. Refrigerate over-night. Serves 10 to 12.

Cures and Curiosities
Keystone Resort

# LOIS'S CHOCOLATE CAKE

| 1-1/2 | cups sugar |
| 1-1/2 | cups mayonnaise |
| 3/4 | cup cocoa |
| 3 | cups flour |
| 1-1/2 | teaspoons baking soda |
| 1-1/2 | cups warm water |
| 1-1/2 | teaspoons vanilla |
| | pinch of salt |

Mix all ingredients together in large mixing bowl. Then beat well with electric mixer. Pour into 2 round cake pans, greased and floured. Bake in a preheated 350 degree oven for 30 to 40 minutes. Test with toothpick and adjust baking time, if necessary until toothpick inserted in center comes out clean. Frost with a good milk chocolate frosting.

Pat Hubbard
Keystone, Colorado

# ELEGANT ORANGE CAKE

3-1/2   cups flour
2   teaspoons baking soda
1/2   teaspoon salt
1/2   cup butter or margarine
1/2   cup shortening
1-1/2   cups sugar
4   eggs
1-1/2   cups buttermilk
2   teaspoons orange extract
1   cup raisins, chopped
1   cup walnuts, chopped
1/3   cup butter or margarine, softened
4   cups (1 pound) powdered sugar
1/4   cup orange juice

*Cake*: Sift together flour, soda and salt, set aside. Cream butter, shortening and sugar in mixing bowl. Gradually beat in eggs and buttermilk alternately with sifted dry ingredients. Add orange extract and blend. Add raisins and nuts. Pour batter into 2, 9-inch cake pans that have been greased and floured. Bake in a preheated 350 degree oven 30 to 35 minutes. Cool for 5 minutes after baking and then turn out onto wire rack to cool completely.

*Frosting*: Beat together the remaining ingredients, adding more juice, if necessary, for creamy spreading consistency.

*You may also add grated orange peel to the cake batter and to garnish frosting.*

Dorothy Bennett
Iowa City, Iowa

# CROWNED CARROT CAKE

| 1 | tablespoon vegetable shortening |
| 3/4 | cup chopped nuts |
| 1-1/2 | cups firmly packed brown sugar |
| 3/4 | cup vegetable oil |
| 4 | eggs |
| 1-1/2 | cups all-purpose flour |
| 1 | cup ground oat flour* |
| 1-1/2 | teaspoons baking powder |
| 1 | teaspoon salt |
| 1 | teaspoon allspice |
| 1 | teaspoon cinnamon |
| 3 | cups shredded carrot |
| 3/4 | cup raisins |
| 1 | 3-ounce package cream cheese, softened |
| 2 | teaspoons lemon juice |
| 1 | cup confectioners' sugar |
| 1 | tablespoon milk |

*Cake:* Generously grease 12-cup bundt or 10-inch tube pan with shortening; coat pan with nuts. Combine sugar and oil; add eggs, one at a time, beating well after each addition. Stir in flour, oat flour, baking powder, salt, allspice and cinnamon. Add carrot and raisins; mix well. Pour into prepared pan; bake in preheated 350-degree oven 45 to 50 minutes or until wooden pick inserted in center comes out clean. Cool 10 minutes; remove from pan. Cool completely on wire rack.

*Frosting:* Beat together cream cheese and lemon juice until well blended. Gradually add sugar and milk, beating until smooth. Makes 1 cup frosting.

*Microwave Directions:* Prepare 12-cup microwave bundt dish as recipe directs. Increase vegetable oil to 1 cup; reduce shredded carrot to 2-1/2 cups. Pour batter into prepared dish; cook in microwave oven on high, 13 to 14 minutes or until wooden pick inserted in center comes out clean, rotating one-quarter turn after each 5 minutes of cooking. Cool 10 to 15 minutes; remove from dish. Cool completely on wire rack.

*Baking powder has already been adjusted for high altitude. It is better not to pack brown sugar. Baking time takes approximately 10 to 15 minutes longer.*

Tammy Moon
Keystone, Colorado

*Place 1 to 1-1/2 cups oatmeal (quick or old fashioned, uncooked) in blender or food processor. Blend or process for about 60 seconds. Store in tightly-covered container in cool, dry place up to six months.

## JANE BERGMAN'S CHRISTMAS BUNDT

|       | butter                        |
|-------|-------------------------------|
|       | sugar                         |
|       | pecans                        |
| 1     | cup shortening                |
| 2     | cups sugar                    |
| 3     | eggs                          |
| 1     | teaspoon salt                 |
| 1     | can evaporated milk           |
| 3-1/2 | cups flour                    |
| 4     | teaspoons baking powder       |
| 2     | teaspoons vanilla             |
| 1     | teaspoon almond flavoring     |
| 2     | teaspoons cinnamon            |
| 1     | cup sugar                     |

Preheat oven to 350 degrees. Butter bundt pan and coat with sugar. Place pecan halves in flutes. Combine next nine ingredients in large bowl and beat with electric mixer for 15 minutes. Pour one-third of batter into pan and sprinkle heavily with mixture of cinnamon and sugar. Repeat layers twice more. Bake for 1 hour and 15 minutes. Do not open oven. Serves 12.

*A favorite!*

Jane Bergman
Cedar Rapids, Iowa

## POPULAR CUPCAKES

|     |                                    |
|-----|------------------------------------|
| 1   | chocolate cake mix                 |
| 1   | 8-ounce package cream cheese       |
| 1/3 | cup sugar                          |
| 1   | egg                                |
|     | dash of salt                       |
| 1   | 6-ounce package chocolate chips    |

Prepare cake mix according to package directions. Fill paper baking cups two-thirds full. Mix softened cream cheese, sugar, egg, salt and chocolate chips together. Drop one teaspoonful of this mixture on the top of each cupcake before baking. Bake at 350 degrees for 15 minutes or according to package directions for cupcakes. Frost with favorite frosting. Makes about 30 cupcakes.

Mrs. Ivan Auer
Naperville, Illinois

# GRANDMA LASCHANZKY'S BULLS EYES (SWEDISH PASTRY)

| | |
|---|---|
| 7 | cardamom seeds, shelled |
| 1 | package dry yeast |
| 1 | quart milk, warmed |
| 1-1/2 | cups sugar |
| 1 | tablespoon salt |
| 2 | tablespoons lard, melted |
| 5 | eggs |
| 4-6 | cups sifted flour |
| 1 | cup raisins |
| | hot water |
| | lard |
| | confectioners' sugar |

Put cardamom seeds into a cloth and pound to crush. Dissolve yeast in milk. Add sugar, salt, lard and eggs. Stir in flour and mix to consistency of pancake batter. In separate bowl cover raisins with hot water to plump. Drain, and add with cardomom seeds to batter. Let dough rise twice, stirring after first rising.

Using Swedish Pastry Pan, put 1 tablespoon lard in each rounded mold of pan. After the first batch of pastries, you will not need as much lard to grease the pan. Over a medium heat, spoon by tablespoons into each mold. Cook until bubbly and turn with a small spatula to brown on the other side. Should be thin with crisp edges and lightly browned.

Put confectioners' sugar into paper bag and gently shake pastries to coat.

Jody and Darrell Laschanzky
Littleton, Colorado

# FINE OATMEAL COOKIES

1     cup sugar
1     cup butter or margarine
2     eggs
1     teaspoon cinnamon
1     teaspoon cloves
1/2    teaspoon salt
1/2    teaspoon baking soda
5     tablespoons milk
2     cups plus 3 tablespoons flour
2     cups Quaker oats
1     cup raisins
1     cup chopped walnuts

Cream sugar and butter. Add eggs. Mix well. Add cinnamon, cloves, salt and baking soda. Mix in milk and flour alternately. Mix in oats, raisins and nuts. Drop by large tablespoons onto an ungreased cookie sheet. Bake at 350 degrees for 10 to 12 minutes. Makes 2 dozen cookies.

*This recipe is over 100 years old. It originated in a boarding house located in the gold mining camp of Goldfield, Nevada.*
Nancy Spencer
Lakewood, Colorado

# GRANDMA PERKINS'S OLD FASHIONED SUGAR COOKIES

1/2    cup butter
1     cup sugar
2     eggs
1     teaspoon baking soda
2     teaspoons baking powder
1/2    teaspoon nutmeg
     pinch of salt
1     cup sour cream
2     cups flour

Cream butter, sugar and eggs. Add dry ingredients except flour. Add sour cream. Then mix in 2 cups flour, using additional flour to roll and cut. Chill dough before rolling. Cut into shapes and frost with red and green frosting for the holidays or any other desired color. Makes 2-1/2 dozen cookies.

*Make a double recipe for holidays.*

Jody and Darrell Laschanzky
Littleton, Colorado

# EASY OLD FASHIONED SUGAR COOKIES

| 1 | cup powdered sugar |
| 1 | cup sugar |
| 1 | cup cooking oil |
| 1 | cup softened margarine |
| 2 | eggs |
| 1 | teaspoon vanilla extract |
| 1 | teaspoon salt |
| 1 | teaspoon baking soda |
| 1 | teaspoon cream of tartar |
| 4 | cups flour |

Cream the sugars, oil and margarine. Beat in the eggs. Add the rest of ingredients. Mix. Chill several hours. Drop small spoonfuls of dough on cookie sheet 2 inches apart. Place some granulated sugar in a bowl, coat bottom of a glass with sugar and mash cookie balls flat. Bake at 375 degrees for 8 minutes. Makes 4 dozen cookies.

*Try to find a glass with a cut-glass bottom.*

Sandy Dabney
Dallas, Texas

# QUICK MOLASSES SUGAR COOKIES

| 3/4 | cup margarine, melted |
| 1 | cup sugar |
| 1/4 | cup molasses |
| 1 | egg, beaten |
| 2 | teaspoons baking powder |
| 2 | cups flour, sifted |
| 1/2 | teaspoon cloves |
| 1/2 | teaspoon ginger |
| 1 | teaspoon cinnamon |
| 1/2 | teaspoon salt |

Cream together margarine, sugar, molasses and egg. Combine remaining ingredients and add to molasses mixture. Mix thoroughly. Chill. Make into walnut-sized balls and roll in sugar. Bake in a preheated 375 degree oven 8 to 10 minutes.

Dorothy Bennett
Iowa City, Iowa

## LEMON BARS

2      cups flour
1      cup margarine
1/2    cup powdered sugar
1/2    cup almonds, lightly browned in dry skillet
1/8    teaspoon salt (optional)
2      cups sugar
4      eggs
6      tablespoons lemon juice
       grated rind of 1 lemon
4      tablespoons flour
1/4    teaspoon salt
1      teaspoon baking powder
       powdered sugar

Put first 5 ingredients into food processor. Process only until lumpy but mixed. Press gently into lightly-greased 13x9-inch pan. Bake at 350 degrees for 20 minutes, or until beginning to brown.

Put next 7 ingredients into food processor. Process until smooth. Pour over hot crust. Bake 25 minutes in 350 degree oven. Sprinkle with powdered sugar. Cover with waxed paper and bring to room temperature before placing in refrigerator to chill.

Judy Miller
Solon, Iowa

## COOKIES AND CREAM DESSERT

1/2    cup butter
1      package Oreo cookies, crushed
1/2    gallon vanilla or peppermint ice cream
1-1/2  cups Spanish peanuts
1/2    cup butter
2      cups powdered sugar
1-1/2  cups evaporated milk
2/3    cup chocolate chips
1      teaspoon vanilla

Melt 1/2 cup butter and mix with crushed Oreo cookies. Spread in a 9x13-inch pan. Spread 1/2 gallon slightly softened ice cream over cookies and top with peanuts. Freeze until firm.

*Sauce:* Melt butter, sugar, evaporated milk and chocolate chips in a saucepan. Boil and stir 8 minutes. Add 1 teaspoon vanilla. Spread over cookie mixture and refreeze. Serves 15.

*Use Oreo cookies only and real butter!*

Jackie Wicklund
Anoka, Minnesota

# MARSHMALLOW FUDGIES

| | |
|---|---|
| 4 | eggs |
| 2 | cups sugar |
| 1/2 | cup flour |
| 1 | teaspoon baking powder |
| 3 | squares unsweetened chocolate, melted |
| 1 | cup butter, melted |
| 1 | cup pecans, broken |
| 2 | teaspoons vanilla |
| 6 | ounces mini-marshmallows |
| 1/2 | cup melted butter |
| 2 | squares unsweetened chocolate, melted |
| 1 | 5-1/3-ounce can evaporated milk |
| 1 | cup sugar |
| 1 | pound confectioners' sugar |
| 1 | teaspoon vanilla |

In a medium-sized mixing bowl, beat eggs and sugar until thick. Sift together flour and baking powder; blend into egg mixture. Mix next 4 ingredients. Spread batter into a well-greased 9x13-inch pan. Bake in a preheated 325 degree oven for 40 minutes or until done. Cover the hot cake with all the mini-marshmallows.

*Topping:* In top of double broiler, mix together 1/2 cup melted butter, chocolate, evaporated milk and sugar. Cook, stirring constantly, until sugar is dissolved. Beat in confectioners' sugar and vanilla. Pour over marshmallow-covered hot cake. Wait until the next day to cut into 2x2-inch squares.

*Store in tightly covered tin canister at room temperature.*

Barbara N. O'Hara
Dayton, Ohio

# CHOCOLAT AU PROVENCE

8       ounces semisweet chocolate
2-1/2   tablespoons butter
1/4     cup sliced strawberries
1/4     cup diced fresh pineapple
1/4     cup diced melon (honeydew or cantaloupe)
1/4     cup diced banana
1/4     cup diced orange
3       tablespoons sugar
3       tablespoons Grand Marnier
        sponge cake cut into 8 rounds, 2 inches in diameter
1/4     cup Grand Marnier
        vanilla ice cream
1       cup heavy cream, whipped to form stiff peaks
8       whole strawberries

Heat chocolate and butter over low heat until chocolate is melted and mixture is smooth. Using a flexible spatula, swirl chocolate around the bottoms and sides of 8 large paper baking cups. Place cups in muffin tins and chill. Peel off the paper and keep refrigerated until ready to use. Mix the fruit with sugar and 3 tablespoons Grand Marnier.

*To assemble*: Put a cake round into the bottom of each chocolate cup. Sprinkle cake rounds evenly, using 1/4 cup Grand Marnier. Put a large spoonful of ice cream over cake and cover with a spoonful of fruit mixture. Garnish with a spoonful of whipped cream and top with a whole strawberry. Serves 8.

Carol Brandt
Newport News, Virginia

135

## GRANDMA'S VANILLA ICE CREAM

| 2 | cups sugar |
|---|---|
| 5 | eggs, beaten |
| 4 | cups milk |
| 5 | cups half and half |
| 5 | teaspoons pure vanilla |
| 1/2 | teaspoon salt |

Add sugar to beaten eggs. Beat until stiff. Add remaining ingredients and mix well. Freeze in 1 gallon ice cream freezer.

Katherine Frost
Englewood, Colorado

## BAKED INDIAN PUDDING

| 1 | teaspoon salt |
|---|---|
| 1/2 | cup yellow corn meal |
| 1 | quart milk |
| 1/4 | cup molasses |
| 1/2 | cup sugar |
| 1/2 | teaspoon cinnamon |
| 1/4 | teaspoon nutmeg |
| 2 | tablespoons butter |

Sprinkle salt over corn meal. Scald 3 cups milk and pour over salted corn meal. Add remaining ingredients except 1 cup milk; mix thoroughly. Place into a 1-1/2-quart buttered casserole. Put casserole into a 250 degree oven. After pudding has been in oven 20 minutes, add remaining cold milk and stir carefully. To ensure proper consistency, stir carefully 4 or 5 times during first 1-1/2 hours of baking. Bake for a total of 5 hours. Serves 6 to 8.

*Serve warm with whipped cream or ice cream.*

Charlotte Wilson Chadima
Cedar Rapids, Iowa

## CHOCOLATE SAUCE

4       tablespoons butter
2       squares unsweetened chocolate
1/4     cup cocoa
3/4     cup sugar
1/2     cup milk
        pinch of salt
1       teaspoon vanilla

Melt butter in a double boiler. Add chocolate squares and stir until melted and smooth. Add cocoa, sugar, milk, salt and vanilla. Stir until boiling.

*Wonderful poured over ice cream, cake, fruit...anything.*

Elra Currie
Belleaire Bluffs, Florida

## FAMOUS HOT FUDGE SAUCE

2       squares chocolate
1/4     cup butter
3/4     cup sugar
1/4     cup cocoa
1/4     teaspoon salt
1       cup cream or large can evaporated milk
1       teaspoon vanilla

Melt chocolate and butter in a saucepan. When nearly melted, add sugar, cocoa and salt. Stir well and add cream; bring to a boil, stirring constantly. Add vanilla. Serve hot or cold. Makes 1-1/2 cups.

Karin Weber
Dallas, Texas

# GINGERBREAD SAUCE

| 1 | cup sugar |
|---|---|
| 1/2 | cup butter |
| 2 | tablespoons flour |
| 1 | egg |
| | juice of one orange |
| 1/2 | cup boiling water |

In saucepan combine all ingredients and stir over medium heat until thickened. Pour over fresh gingerbread.

Betty Coddington
Humboldt, Iowa

# NEVER FAIL CANDY

| 1/4 | pound butter or margarine |
|---|---|
| 4 | cups sugar |
| 1 | can evaporated milk |
| 1 | pint jar marshmallow cream |
| 1 | 16-ounce package chocolate chips |
| 1 | cup chopped nuts |

Combine butter, sugar and evaporated milk in a saucepan and boil until a candy thermometer reaches 238 degrees. Add the marshmallow cream, chocolate chips and nuts. Stir until well mixed. Pour into a greased 9x13-inch pan. Cool and cut into squares.

*To make peanut butter candy, substitute peanut butter chips for chocolate chips.*

Helen B. Davis
Orient, Iowa

## CHOCOLATE BON BONS

| | |
|---|---|
| 1 | 12-ounce package chocolate chips |
| 1 | can sweetened condensed milk |
| 2 | cups graham cracker crumbs |
| 1 | cup raisins |
| 3/4 | cup chopped nuts |
| 1 | teaspoon vanilla extract |
| | coconut (optional) |
| | graham cracker crumbs (optional) |

Melt chocolate, remove from heat and add next 5 ingredients. Mix well and form into balls. Roll in graham cracker crumbs or coconut or just leave plain.

*I melt the chocolate chips in my microwave oven, for a total of 3 minutes (1-1/2 minutes, turn, then another 1-1/2 minutes). As oven temperatures vary, be sure and check after 1-1/2 minutes.*

Jody Laschanzky
Littleton, Colorado

## CREAM CANDY

| | |
|---|---|
| 1 | can evaporated milk |
| 1 | cup corn syrup |
| 3 | cups sugar |
| 1 | tablespoon vanilla |
| 1 | cup chopped nuts |

Combine evaporated milk, corn syrup and sugar in a saucepan and slowly bring to a boil. Stir constantly until 236 degrees on a candy thermometer. Cool to lukewarm and add vanilla and nuts. Beat candy until it holds its shape. Turn into greased 9x9-inch pan. Cool and cut into squares. Makes 36 pieces.

Helen B. Davis
Orient, Iowa

# PEANUT BRITTLE

| 1-1/3 | cups raw Spanish peanuts |
| 1 | cup sugar |
| 3/4 | cup white corn syrup |
| 2/3 | cup water |
| 2 | tablespoons butter |
| 2 | teaspoons vanilla |
| 1/2 | teaspoon baking soda |

Warm nuts in a 225 degree oven while making syrup. Boil sugar, corn syrup and water to 265 degrees on a candy thermometer or until a drop spins fine threads. Do not undercook or candy will be sticky. Add butter and nuts. Continue cooking until a golden brown, stirring constantly. Aroma of nuts will be noticeable. Remove from heat; add vanilla and soda. Spread thin on a buttered cookie sheet before candy cools. Break into pieces when cold.

Lorraine M. Lee                    Lakewood, Colorado

# BEER NUTS (MAPLE SUGAR COATED PEANUTS)

| 1-1/2 | cups sugar |
| 3/4 | cup water |
| 1/2 | teaspoon maple flavoring |
| 24 | ounces raw peanuts |
| | salt to taste |

Put sugar, water, maple flavoring and peanuts into an electric frying pan (preferably non-stick). Boil on medium setting, stirring constantly until all moisture is absorbed by the peanuts and the bottom of the pan is dry. Pour the nuts into a greased jelly roll pan. Salt to taste. Bake in a preheated 325 degree oven for 25 minutes, stirring every 8 minutes.

*This inexpensive snack is a real hit with "nibblers".*

Bettie Hunchis                    Edina, Minnesota

## SALTED NUT BARS

| | |
|---|---|
| 3 | cups flour |
| 1/2 | cup brown sugar |
| 1 | teaspoon salt |
| 1 | cup butter or margarine |
| 2 | cups mixed nuts (no Brazils) |
| 1 | cup light corn syrup |
| 2 | tablespoons butter |
| 1 | tablespoon water |
| 1 | 6-ounce package butterscotch chips |

Combine first 4 ingredients and blend well. Press into ungreased 15x10-inch jelly roll pan. Bake 10 to 12 minutes at 350 degrees. Take from oven and top with 2 cups mixed nuts.

Combine remaining ingredients in a small saucepan. Boil 2 minutes, stirring constantly. Pour over nuts. Return to oven and bake 10 minutes more. Cool completely and cut into 48 bars.

Marjorie C. Schnacke
Topeka, Kansas

## FRENCH CHOCOLATE TRUFFLES

| | |
|---|---|
| 1/2 | pound semi-sweet chocolate (Swiss or French is best) |
| 1/3 | cup heavy cream |
| 1/3 | cup unsalted butter |
| 2 | large egg yokes |
| | unsweetened cocoa |

Melt chocolate with cream in top of double boiler, stirring until smooth. Add butter and stir until creamy. Blend in egg yolks. Chill until firm. Take 1 teaspoonful of mixture and roll into a ball. Then roll in cocoa. Place in paper bonbon cups. Chill or freeze. Makes 2-1/2 dozen.

Barb Bell
Iowa City, Iowa

## MOUNTAIN DELIGHT'S CHOCOLATE PIZZA

| 8 | ounces white confectionery coating, chopped |
| 8 | ounces semi-sweet chocolate chips |
| 1/2 | cup miniature marshmallows |
| 1/2 | cup salted peanuts |
| 1/2 | cup crisp rice cereal |
| 1/2 | cup flaked coconut |
| 1/2 | cup M&M's |

Place 6 ounces white confectionery coating and chocolate chips in the top of a double boiler and stir until completely melted. Remove from heat. Add marshmallows, peanuts and rice cereal. Mix well. On a waxed paper lined cookie sheet, spread mixture in a 10-inch circle. Mixture should be approximately 1/2-inch thick. Sprinkle mixture with coconut. While warm, sprinkle M&M's over pizza. In the top of a double boiler melt the remaining 2 ounces of white confectionery coating, stirring. Drizzle over top of pizza to give a cheese appearance. Chill until firm. Break into pieces to serve. Makes approximately 24 pieces.

*Be creative at Christmas time and make a wreath or tree. Tint coconut with green food coloring. Use just green and red M&Ms or green and red candied cherries cut in half to decorate wreath or tree.*

Phil Shive
Iowa City, Iowa

## BAKED CARAMEL CORN

| 2 | cups brown sugar |
| 1 | cup butter or margarine |
| 1/8 | teaspoon cream of tartar |
| 1/2 | cup light corn syrup |
| 1 | teaspoon baking soda |
| 7 | quarts popped corn |
| 1 | cup peanuts (optional) |

Combine first 4 ingredients in a medium-sized saucepan. Bring to a boil over medium-high heat. Boil for 4 to 5 minutes. Remove from heat. Stir in baking soda until well blended. Pour over popped corn and toss to coat. Arrange on cookie sheets. Bake on top rack in a preheated 200 to 225 degree oven for 1 hour. Stir or turn caramel corn every 15 minutes. Store in airtight containers.

*If caramel corn with nuts is desired, mix nuts with popped corn prior to coating with caramel mixture.*

Ellen Borchers
Pueblo, Colorado

**BEVERAGES**

## WASSAIL

| | |
|---|---|
| 6-8 | tea bags |
| 3 | quarts boiling water |
| 1 | pint hot water |
| 2 | cups sugar |
| 2 | teaspoons whole cloves |
| 4 | cinnamon sticks |
| 2-1/2 | gallons apple cider |
| 3 | quarts orange juice |
| 1 | quart grapefruit juice |
| 1 | pint cranberry juice |
| | white wine |

Drape tea bags in boiling water and steep 5 to 7 minutes. In saucepan, stir 1 pint hot water and 2 cups sugar to boiling, dissolving sugar to make syrup. Tie cloves and cinnamon sticks in spice bag. Combine tea, syrup and spice bag with all but wine and refrigerate. Can be prepared the day before event and heated to just simmering point before serving. After reheating to serve, add wine to taste.

Jane Bergman
Cedar Rapids, Iowa

## SPRING FLINGS

| | |
|---|---|
| 1 | bottle Moet Chandon White Star champagne (or your favorite) |
| 2 | cups orange juice |
| 2 | cups pineapple juice |

Fill blender half way with ice. Add half of the orange and pineapple juices. Blend until slushy (like spring snow!) **Slowly** add champagne and stir. Fill almost to the top of blender. Blend one more time to mix. Pour into Margarita glasses or champagne flutes. Repeat with rest of juice and champagne. Use orange and pineapple slices as garnish.

*You may add champagne to mixture in glasses but be careful or it will all fizz out! Great for brunch with "Peru Creek Omelet"! (See Entrees.)*

Snowflake Shop
Keystone Resort

## HOMEMADE BAILEY'S IRISH CREAM

| 3 | eggs |
| 1 | 14-ounce can sweetened condensed milk |
| 3 | tablespoons cream of coconut |
| 4 | ounces milk chocolate, melted (can use plain chocolate bars) |
| 1 | pint light cream |
| 1 | pint heavy cream |
| 1 | pint Canadian whiskey |

Place eggs in a blender and beat well. Add condensed milk, coconut cream and chocolate. Blend at medium speed. Pour contents into a 1/2-gallon container and add light cream, heavy cream and whiskey. Shake or stir well. Pour half of recipe back into blender and mix at medium speed for 30 seconds. Repeat with other half. Combine and refrigerate over-night.

*Bailey's is great in coffee—especially after dinner—or over ice cream or pound cake. Try a "shillelagh"...you know...that Irish walking stick—it's half Bailey's and half Irish Mist.*

Anthony C. Checco
Silverthorne, Colorado

## KAHLUA

| 2 | cups water |
| 3 | cups sugar |
| 1/4 | cup instant coffee |
| 1 | cup hot water |
| 1 | fifth of vodka |
| 1 | 8-inch vanilla bean, split lengthwise |

Simmer 2 cups water and sugar 30 minutes. In separate container, dissolve instant coffee in 1 cup hot water. When sugar mixture is ready, add coffee. Bring to boil. Cool. Pour into 1/2-gallon jug and add vodka and vanilla bean. Let stand three weeks.

*From my mother in Caseville, Michigan. Worth the wait!*

Pat Hubbard
Keystone, Colorado

## PILGRIM'S PROGRESS

1     16-ounce bottle cranberry juice
18    ounces pineapple juice
     lemon slices

Mix cranberry and pineapple juices in large pitcher, pour over crushed ice in three tall glasses, garnish with lemon slices.

*Good punch to use with "Ice Float". (Recipe follows.)*

Polly Shive Pagliai
Iowa City, Iowa

## ICE FLOAT

To keep your punch cold, take a round gelatin mold and cover bottom 1/2-inch with water. Places slices of lemon and/or orange on bottom...in water. Add maraschino cherries for color. Freeze. After frozen, top with water until mold is one-half to two-thirds full. Freeze again. When ready to serve punch, take a wet, hot towel and wipe outside of mold to loosen ice. Turn over into punch.

*You can use Kool-Aid (I use sugar-free) for more color, and any number of different fruits instead of orange or lemon. Use your imagination! I've even seen flowers used!*

Polly Shive Pagliai
Iowa City, Iowa

# HOT CRANBERRY PUNCH

| | |
|---|---|
| 2 | cups water |
| 3/4 | cup sugar |
| 4 | sticks cinnamon |
| 1 | quart cranberry juice cocktail |
| 1 | 6-ounce can frozen orange juice |
| 1 | 6-ounce can frozen lemonade |
| 1 | quart water |

Simmer water, sugar and cinnamon sticks for 10 minutes. Remove cinnamon. Add cranberry juice cocktail, orange juice, lemonade and rest of water. Mix and serve warm.

*Warms you to your toes after a long day of skiing.*

Kay Shive
Solon, Iowa

# HOT CIDER

| | |
|---|---|
| 2 | quarts apple cider |
| 3 | sticks cinnamon |
| 1 | teaspoon salt (optional) |
| 3/4 | cup brown sugar |
| 1 | teaspoon whole cloves |

Heat cider to boiling and add other ingredients. Simmer for 15 minutes; strain before serving. Serve in a mug with a slice of orange.

*This is delicious served as above. Can also add 1 jigger of schnapps to each mug if desired.*

Kay Shive
Solon, Iowa

# RESTAURANTS

The Robert Trent Jones, Jr. championship golf course at Keystone Ranch.

## ALPENTOP DELI, RESTAURANT, BAKERY

At last! A deli with the warm, friendly atmosphere of a European cafe, with cozy table service for breakfast, lunch and dinner. The Alpentop is also Summit County's most complete deli and bakery, with an extensive selection of cheeses, meats, salads, croissants and pastries. Their delivery and catering services are welcome when you're hosting a party, planning a meeting or presenting a basket or tray of gourmet food items.

Breakfast at Alpentop, from 7:00 to 11:00 a.m., features French toast, omelets, Belgian waffles, bagels, croissants, fresh squeezed orange juice and French Roast coffee.

Sandwiches, available from 7:00 a.m. to 9:00 p.m., include a variety of cheeses, meats, sprouts and tomatoes on croissants, French, wheat or rye breads. Enjoy your sandwich there or have it prepared to take with you.

Lunch also features wonderful fresh soups, chowders, chili, a daily chef's special and deli case salads. For dessert, try one of the Alpentop's famous chocolate chip or oatmeal raisin cookies, fresh from the oven.

Enjoy a cocktail while you relax at dinner, from 5:00 to 9:00 p.m., offering you a choice of appetizers and soup d'jour, with a range of entrees from light sandwiches and salad plates to Alpentop's rich stew or chili. Each evening, the chef prepares a special gourmet entree and dessert, providing a delightfully different surprise every day!

In addition, the Alpentop's special fare includes gift baskets, specially decorated birthday cakes, holiday dinners and individually-prepared trays of gourmet cheeses, meats, pate, mousse, hors d'oeuvres, desserts and pastries.

This personalized selection of deli, bakery and gourmet items, plus the warm, friendly atmosphere, give the Alpentop a comfortable touch of home.

## PROVINCIAL TORTE

| | |
|---|---|
| 1 | pound cream cheese |
| 3/4 | pound butter |
| 1-1/2 | pounds flour |
| 1 | egg, beaten |
| 2-1/2 | pounds spinach, torn |
| 1 | clove garlic |
| | pepper, freshly ground, to taste |
| 3 | medium onions, chopped |
| 5 | red peppers, sliced |
| 3 | pounds ham, sliced thin |
| 1 | pound Cheddar cheese, sliced |

Combine cream cheese, butter and flour until dough is not sticky. Chill. Divide dough in half. Roll out each half to fit 9-inch springform pan. Place bottom crust into pan. Egg wash crust. Saute in butter in 3 separate pans, the spinach (with garlic and freshly ground pepper), onions, and red peppers.

Layer ingredients as follows: spinach, onions, peppers, ham, cheese, spinach, onions. Put remaining crust on top and seal with egg wash. Set pan on top of cookie sheet when baking. Bake at 325 degrees for 45 minutes. Serves 10 to 12.

## ALPENTOP WHOLE WHEAT BREAD

| | |
|---|---|
| 1-1/2 | tablespoons dry yeast |
| 1-1/2 | tablespoons honey |
| 3/4 | cup water |
| 2 | eggs |
| 3/4 | cup honey |
| 3-3/4 | cups water |
| 1-1/2 | tablespoons salt |
| 1/3 | cup butter |
| 13 | cups whole wheat flour |

Combine yeast, the 1-1/2 tablespoons honey and water. Allow to grow. Add eggs, 3/4 cup honey, water, salt, butter and whole wheat flour. Knead for 13 minutes. Allow to rise, then punch down. Shape loaves and allow to rise again. Bake for 20 to 25 minutes. Makes 3 loaves.

# CHOCOLATE PEAR TART

| | |
|---|---|
| 1-2/3 | cups all-purpose flour |
| 1/4 | cup sugar |
| 1/2 | teaspoon salt |
| 1-1/4 | sticks butter, chilled and cut into pieces |
| 2 | egg yolks |
| 1 | teaspoon vanilla extract |
| 2 | teaspoons cold water |
| 2 | ounces unsweetened chocolate |
| 1/4 | pound butter |
| 1/2 | cup honey |
| 4 | whole pears |
| 1 | cup sugar |
| 2 | cups red wine |
| 4 | cups water |
| 1/4 | cup apricot glaze |

Sift flour, sugar and salt into a bowl. Cut chilled butter into flour mixture until mixture resembles a course meal. Stir egg yolks, vanilla and water together and add to the flour mixture and blend using a fork. Shape dough into a ball. Chill. Roll dough out between 2 sheets of waxed paper, large enough to line your pan. Weight paper down with beans or rice. Bake at 425 degrees for 10 minutes until edges are brown and remove waxed paper and weight. Combine in a double boiler the chocolate, butter and honey. Cook until well blended. Allow to cool to room temperature. Peel, core and poach pears in sugar, wine and water until tender. Allow to cool. Cut pears in a fan shape, leaving small end intact. Spread chocolate mixture in tart crust. Chocolate should cover entire crust. Lay pears on top of chocolate, fanned out. Heat apricot glaze and pour over pears. Serves 8.

## ARAPAHOE BASIN MIDWAY BARBEQUE

Arapahoe Basin was built in 1946 by Max Dercum and some of his skiing buddies to provide expert ski terrain at an elevation higher than that of any other ski area in the country. On cold, wintry days, you can enjoy hot, spicy chili, homemade soups or a "Burrito Special" at the Arapahoe Basin Midway Barbeque. Or . . . on sunny spring days sample charcoal-broiled cheese-burgers, ribs, chicken and cold beer. Either way, there are always open deck chairs provided for your sun-tanning pleasure and

## OLD FASHIONED BEEF STEW

| | |
|---|---|
| 2 | pounds stew meat |
| | flour to dredge |
| | bacon grease |
| | vegetable oil |
| 1 | medium onion, coarsely diced |
| 1 | cup chopped celery |
| 3/4 | teaspoon garlic concentrate |
| | beef stock or water |
| 2 | tablespoons powdered beef base |
| 1/8 | teaspoon thyme |
| 1/8 | teaspoon rosemary |
| 1 | bay leaf |
| 1 | large carrot, sliced |
| 5 | medium potatoes, quartered and sliced |
| | rice flour |

Dredge beef lightly in flour. Brown in bacon grease, adding oil as necessary. Add onion, celery and garlic. Saute. Cover with beef stock or water and add beef base to taste. Add season-ings. Simmer for 2 hours. Steam carrots and potatoes separ-ately. Remove bay leaf from beef soup and thicken with white-wash of rice flour. Add vegetables and adjust seasonings. Serves 6.

## BENTLEY'S

Bentley's has a history as long as Keystone Resort itself. It was developed as a relaxing cocktail lounge with a unique art deco decor by one of Keystone's earliest characters, Malcom Clark. The decor was based on the exploits of W. O. Bentley and his fantastic automobile. From its beginning, Bentley's has enjoyed bringing a different mood to Keystone with its cosmopolitan flair, speciality drinks, large sunny deck overlooking the lake and—great food.

When the ownership of Bentley's was transferred to Walter Awada in 1978, he addressed the need for increased dining accommodation. At that time a kitchen was added and a modest menu of burgers, soups and sandwiches was designed. Since that time this menu has been constantly changed and adapted to meet the unique desires of our wide-reaching clientele.

Many guests have left Keystone with one of their fondest memories being the Colorado sunshine, a refreshing cocktail and the boaters or skaters on the lake as viewed from the year-round deck at Bentley's. Some of *our* fondest memories at Bentley's are the variety of young people who have worked here while enjoying their Colorado adventure. Many of those who have moved back to their homes throughout the United States, Canada, England and Australia keep in touch and return to visit us years later.

At Bentley's our objective is to make your "dining out" experience a special one. Our primary emphasis is on quality, excellence and good service. Every item on our menu is prepared with the finest ingredients available, carefully hand-selected and prepared daily to ensure the highest quality. Breakfast is served seasonally from 7:00 to 10:30 a.m., lunch from 11:00 a.m. to 5:00 p.m. and dinner from 5:00 to 10:00 p.m. We hope you enjoy your experience at Bentley's while visiting beautiful Keystone Resort.

# MUDD PIE

| | |
|---|---|
| 1 | cup chocolate fudge sauce |
| 2 | prepared chocolate cookie pie shells |
| 1 | pint Butter Brickle ice cream |
| 1 | pint Coffee ice cream |
| | whipped cream |

Heat fudge sauce; pour half into each pie shell. Refrigerate until firm. Mix ice creams together but do not allow to soften completely. When fudge has hardened, fill pie shells with ice cream and freeze. Top with whipped cream. Serves 12.

# POPPY SEED DRESSING

| | |
|---|---|
| 1/4 | cup sugar |
| 1 | teaspoon dry mustard |
| 1 | teaspoon salt |
| 1/3 | cup white vinegar |
| 1/4 | cup finely-grated onions |
| 1 | cup salad oil |
| 1-1/2 | tablespoons poppy seeds |
| 1 | egg |

Mix all ingredients well. Makes 2 cups.

*Delicious over fruit as well as green salad.*

# TERIYAKI CHICKEN

| | |
|---|---|
| 1/4 | cup honey |
| 1/4 | cup soy sauce |
| 1 | teaspoon ginger |
| 1 | teaspoon garlic powder |
| 1-1/3 | cups dry white wine |
| 4 | 10-ounce chicken breasts, boned |
| 4 | pineapple rings |

Heat honey. Mix soy sauce, ginger, garlic powder and wine. Brush chicken breasts with warm honey and place in marinade. Let marinate 1 hour. Place chicken breasts in shallow pan and top with pineapple rings. Bake at 375 degrees for 15 minutes. Serves 4.

## BIGHORN STEAKHOUSE

Located within the Keystone Lodge, the Bighorn Steakhouse is an elegant western, cozy dining room where the warm color schemes, comfortable booth seating and friendly service complement mouthwatering steaks, seafood, poultry and Summit County's favorite salad bar which features 28 items including freshly baked bread. Dining hours are Sunday through Thursday, 5:30 to 10:00 p.m.; Friday and Saturday, 5:30 to 10:30 p.m. No reservations are necessary.

## BROILED SCALLOPS WITH GARLIC AND CHEESE BREAD CRUMBS

2       pounds scallops
1       cup dry white wine (Chablis, Chenin Blanc or
            Sauvignon Blanc)
        juice of 2 lemons
4       tablespoons butter, 1/2-inch pieces
4       tablespoons butter, melted
2       cloves garlic, minced
2       tablespoons chopped parsley
        salt and pepper to taste
1       cup fine bread crumbs
2       tablespoons Parmesan cheese

Clean scallops; rinse lightly and remove any small muscular "feet" attached to the side of the scallops. Place in 1-1/2 to 2-quart flat casserole without stacking scallops. Pour white wine over scallops to depth half height of scallops. Sprinkle lemon juice and butter pieces over the top. Bake uncovered at 350 degrees for 10 minutes.

Meanwhile, prepare bread crumb mixture. Saute melted butter and garlic for 2 minutes; toss together with parsley, salt, pepper, bread crumbs and Parmesan cheese. Cover scallops with the bread crumb mixture and finish cooking (10 minutes). Bread crumbs should turn golden.
*Serve with a rich Sauvignon Blanc or Chardonnay.*

## FILET MIGNON

2       egg yolks
8       ounces warm, clarified butter
1/8     teaspoon cayenne
1       tablespoon lemon juice
        salt to taste
4       7-ounce butterflied filet mignon, or steak of your
            choice
8       1/4-inch slices Canadian bacon
8       artichoke hearts
8       1/2-inch onion rings, crisply fried

Prepare hollandaise sauce by whipping egg yolks over low flame or in top of double boiler until lemon-yellow in color and almost fluffy. Slowly add warm butter in a stream and whisk continually to combine with yolks. Add cayenne, lemon juice and salt. Set aside.

Broil or grill steaks to individual preference. Five minutes before steaks are done, heat Canadian bacon and artichoke hearts in saute pan or microwave.

To assemble, place 1 slice Canadian bacon, 1 artichoke heart and 1 onion ring on top of steak. Pour 2 tablespoons hollandaise sauce into onion ring.

*Serve with a rich Cabernet Sauvignon or Merlot wine.*

## EDGEWATER CAFE

Formerly the Brasserie, the Edgewater Cafe sits on the edge of the Keystone Lake and looks upon the Continental Divide. Our family restaurant features hearty breakfasts, lunches and a variety of dinner entrees. Cafe seasonal hours are 6:30 a.m. to 9:00 p.m.

## FRENCH ONION SOUP

| | |
|---|---|
| 4 | tablespoons butter, margarine or oil |
| 5 | pounds yellow onions, sliced 1/4-inch thick |
| 1 | cup dry red wine |
| 2 | cloves fresh garlic, minced |
| 1/4 | teaspoon white pepper |
| 1 | teaspoon thyme |
| 1 | bay leaf |
| 2 | cans beef bouillon |
| 3 | quarts homemade chicken stock |
| | toasted crouton rounds cut from loaf bread to fit serving bowl |
| | provolone cheese (2 ounces per portion), grated |

In a 1-1/4-gallon pot, warm butter, margarine or oil; brown onions until they begin to caramelize. . .almost until one-quarter are "burnt". Deglaze pan with wine, stirring up caramelized onion from pan. Add garlic. Add next 5 ingredients Simmer, partially covered, for 2 hours.

Pour soup into bowl, top with a crouton and 2 ounces provolone cheese. Melt under broiler until cheese bubbles.

*Serve with a Chardonnay or Merlot wine. Freezes nicely.*

## RUM BATTER FRENCH TOAST

| | |
|---|---|
| 3 | eggs, beaten |
| 1/4 | cup dark rum or brandy |
| 1-1/2 | cups milk or half and half |
| 2 | tablespoons white or brown sugar |
| 1/8 | teaspoon nutmeg |
| 8-12 | slices 1-inch raisin or French bread |
| | butter or oil to saute French toast |
| 1 | stick butter or margarine, softened |
| 4 | tablespoons orange or apricot marmalade |
| 2 | tablespoons dark rum |
| | powdered sugar to garnish |

*French Toast:* Whip eggs, rum, milk, sugar and nutmeg. Pour batter into a casserole dish. Soak slices of bread until saturated, approximately 3 minutes. Melt butter or oil on griddle; saute bread until golden on both sides. Serve with orange marmalade butter (see below) and powdered sugar garnish.

*Marmalade Butter:* Whip butter until light and creamy, add marmalade and rum. Blend well.

# Garden Room Restaurant

## GARDEN ROOM

The Garden Room opened in December of 1974 with Jack Bench as Executive Chief. A deck was added in 1976 and later was enclosed with a green house. The interior space concept was totally redone in 1980—booths were added, beautiful wood paneling from floor to ceiling, as well as leaded glass.

Mr. and Mrs. Erickson designed the original room and all subsequent upgrades. The intent was to provide a unique hotel dining room to the Colorado mountains which took advantage of the sun and view, gave a sense of warmth and friendliness and provided cuisine that was exceptional for the locale.

There is belief that the success and uniqueness of a resort is in the food and staff. Freshness of ingredients is paramount and we try to take advantage of longer-term trends while, at the same time, maintaining traditional favorites. Dining hours are Sunday through Thursday, 6:00 to 9:30 p.m.; Friday and Saturday, 6:00 to 10:00 p.m. Reservations are suggested.

# VEAL WITH PISTACHIO AND
# TOMATO BASIL SAUCE

| | |
|---|---|
| 1/4 | cup flour |
| 1/4 | cup finely ground pistachio nuts |
| 2 | egg yolks |
| 1/2 | cup milk |
| 4 | 6-ounce servings veal loin or cutlet prepared by your butcher |
| 2 | cloves garlic, minced |
| 6 | tablespoons clarified butter or oil |
| 1 | cup dry red wine |
| 1 | 12-ounce can crushed tomatoes |
| 2 | tablespoons fresh basil, diced (or 1-1/2 teaspoons dried) |
| 2 | tablespoons butter or oil |
| 2 | tablespoons Parmesan cheese to garnish |

Mix flour and nuts. In a separate dish, blend egg yolks and milk. Dip veal into egg-milk mixture, then dredge in flour-nut mixture.

Prepare tomato basil sauce by simmering garlic and 6 tablespoons butter for 2 minutes. Add red wine; simmer 1 minute. Add tomatoes and basil. Simmer an additional 10 minutes.

In saute pan, warm 2 tablespoons butter or oil and lightly brown veal on medium flame until golden on both sides—approximately 2 minutes.

Place sauce in a pond on plate. Top with one portion of veal and sprinkle with fresh Parmesan cheese. Serves 4.

*Serve with a California Pinot Noir or Merlot.*

# SHRIMP DIJON

| 2 | pounds shrimp; peeled, deveined, butterflied |
| 4 | tablespoons clarified butter |
| 3 | shallots, diced |
|   | white wine |
| 3 | tablespoons country-style Dijon mustard |
| 1 | cup half and half or heavy cream |

In 3-quart saute pan, saute shrimp in clarified butter until opaque, or half cooked. Add shallots; cook 30 seconds. Deglaze pan with white wine. Reduce liquid to half, so that approximately 1/4 cup liquid remains. Add Dijon mustard and cream. Simmer until shrimp are firm. Do not overcook.

*Serve with rice and a green vegetable and a nice California Sauvignon Blanc or Chardonnay.*

# The GREATEST CREPE

## GREATEST CREPE WAGON

During my travels through France I became fascinated with an individual behind a 15-inch crepe grill who performed an artistic show while creating a folded Grand Marnier, sugar or chocolate crepe. Feeling the need to introduce this wonderful cuisine to the United States, I purchased my first 70-pound grill.

I incorporated the 15-inch double French grill platter into a hand crafted, 10- by 9- by 6-foot oak, brass and copper wagon. In the summer it was located in the Keystone Plaza and in the winter moved to the ski area. During the winter of 1983-84, I elected to remain at the ski area and only operate during the ski season.

After several years of being called "the Greatest Creep", people now appreciate the artistic show of creating a 15-inch, authentic French crepe.—*Helen Burrack*

## CREPE-A-DILLA (as in Mexican Quesadilla)

| | |
|---|---|
| 1/3 | cup oil |
| 3/4 | cup water |
| 2 | caps Real Lemon Juice Concentrate |
| 1/4 | cup sugar |
| 1 | cup whole wheat flour |
| 1-1/2 | cups unbleached white, high altitude flour |
| 10 | eggs |
| 3-1/2 | cups whole milk |
| | butter |
| | blend of shredded Cheddar and mozzarella cheeses |
| | sliced Jalapeno peppers |
| | hot and sweet honey mustard |

*Batter:* Mix in blender the first 8 ingredients in order listed. Blend 1 minute on high. Scrape down sides. Blend another 15 seconds on high. Pour into 2, 1-quart containers. Refrigerate for not less than 1 hour—preferably prepared the night before. Makes 2 quarts.

*Filling:* Heat crepe grill or pan. When a sprinkle of water sizzles, pour 1/2 cup of batter onto the grill or pan. Cook on one side and turn over. Squeeze a circle of butter, sprinkle on cheese to cover crepe. Add peppers to individual's taste. Add a little mustard. Wait until cheese melts, then roll up and serve. Makes 12, 15-inch crepes or 24, 8-inch crepes.

# BRATWURST WITH CHEESE AND SAUERKRAUT

| 1/3 | cup oil |
| 3/4 | cup water |
| 2 | caps Real Lemon Juice Concentrate |
| 1/4 | cup sugar |
| 1 | cup whole wheat flour |
| 1-1/2 | cups unbleached white high altitude flour |
| 10 | eggs |
| 3-1/2 | cups whole milk |
| | butter |
| | blend of shredded Cheddar and mozzarella cheeses |
| | hot and sweet honey mustard |
| | 15-inch bratwurst, cooked and drained |
| | sauerkraut, heated |

*Batter:* Mix in a blender the first 8 ingredients in order listed. Blend for 1 minute on high. Scrape down sides. Blend another 15 seconds on high. Pour into 2, 1-quart containers. Refrigerate for not less than 1 hour—preferably prepared the night before. Makes 2 quarts.

*Filling:* Heat grill or pan. When a sprinkle of water sizzles, pour 1/2 cup of batter onto the surface. Cook on one side and turn over. Squeeze a circle of butter, sprinkle on cheese to cover crepe. Add mustard. Lay bratwurst lengthwise. Roll up crepe. Put sauerkraut on top. Add more mustard to taste. Makes 12, 15-inch crepes or 24, 8-inch crepes.

# KAHLUA-BANANA CREPE

| | |
|---|---|
| 1/3 | cup oil |
| 3/4 | cup water |
| 2 | caps Real Lemon Juice Concentrate |
| 1/4 | cup sugar |
| 1 | cup whole wheat flour |
| 1-1/2 | cups unbleached white high altitude flour |
| 10 | eggs |
| 3-1/2 | cups whole milk |
| | butter |
| | nuts (sundae nut topping) |
| 1 | whole banana cut into eighths |
| 1 | ounce Kahlua |
| | whipped cream or powdered sugar for garnish |

*Batter:* Mix in blender the first 8 ingredients in order listed. Blend for 1 minute on high. Scrape down sides. Blend another 15 seconds on high. Pour into 2, 1-quart containers. Refrigerate for not less than 1 hour- preferably prepared the night before. Makes 2 quarts.

*Filling:* Heat grill or pan. When a sprinkle of water sizzles, pour 1/2 cup of batter onto grill. When crepe is done on one side, turn crepe over, add a little squeeze of butter or margarine and a sprinkle of nuts. Lay the banana slices lengthwise; add 1 ounce of Kahlua. Let set for 15 seconds. Roll crepe and serve with whipped cream or powdered sugar. Makes 12, 15-inch crepes or 24, 8-inch crepes.

## KEYSTONE RANCH

Keystone Ranch is rich in history and the tradition of the Old West. Before the white man came to settle, the Ute and Arapaho Indians made this area their summer campground—fishing and hunting the plentiful buffalo. In the early 1870s, settlers drifted into the valley. Luke E. Smith, son of one of the original homesteaders in the area, acquired the three original homesteads of the valley and, in 1938, established a working cattle ranch that remained active until 1972. Now the site of the Keystone Ranch Golf Course, the valley is surrounded by mountains. To the east is Keystone Mountain; to the south are Mt. Geogh, Mt. Baldy, and Silver Heels; and to the north and west the panorama of the Ten Mile and Gore Ranges unfolds. Trout Creek, running through the valley from south to north, is a natural spawning ground for native mountain trout.

In the clubhouse living room, the fireplace is original and was a wedding gift to Mr. Smith's daughter, Bernadine, when she married Howard H. Reynolds. The living room was constructed of pine logs from nearby Keystone Mountain, and more rooms were added later to accommodate the many friends and business associates who came here to enjoy their summers in the mountains. The wing that houses the bar and clubhouse facilities has been added recently, and the original decor has been retained by use of appointments reminiscent of the area's rustic past and Western heritage. First seating is from 6:00 to 7:00 p.m. and second seating is from 8:15 to 9:00 p.m. Reservations required.

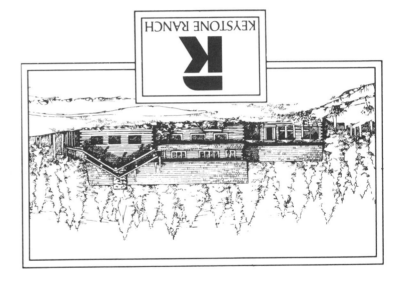

KEYSTONE RANCH

# FRESH MUSSELS WITH PASTA

| | |
|---|---|
| 1 | dozen New Zealand Green Lip Mussels |
| 1/2 | teaspoon minced fresh garlic |
| 1 | teaspoon minced fresh basil |
| 1/2 | cup olive oil |
| 1 | cup dry white wine |
| 1 | cup heavy whipping cream |
| 1/4 | cup tomato, diced small |
| | pinch of fennel seed |
| 1/2 | lime, juiced |
| | salt, white pepper, cayenne to taste |
| | cornstarch (optional) |
| | cooked pasta of your choice |
| 1/2 | cup grated Parmesan cheese |

Scrub mussels on outside and remove the "beard". Heat a 3-quart pan or one which will easily hold the 12 mussels, which are fairly large. If you use the smaller black domestic mussels, provide at least 6 per serving.

Saute the garlic and basil in the olive oil, taking care not to let the garlic brown and become bitter. Add the mussels, wine, cream, tomato and fennel seed. Cover and let steam for 5 minutes or until most of the mussels have opened their shells. Do not overcook.

Remove the mussels from the sauce and then remove the mussels from the shells. Save a couple of half-shells for garnish.

Reduce the sauce to approximately 3 cups. . .the mussels will have provided some juice. . .seasoning with the lime juice, salt, white pepper (careful) and cayenne (extra careful) to taste. Tighten with cornstarch if needed. Add the cooked pasta of your choice. We use a saffron linguini which gives a yellow look to the dish. Add mussels.

With the pan off the fire, add the grated Parmesan and serve with the shell and a spring of basil as garnish.

*This is a small appetizer. If you have big eaters or a small entree, you may serve this recipe for 3 or 4 people. As a practical matter, you may like to prepare everything prior to adding the pasta ahead of time, completing the dish at the time of service. Remember to add the Parmesan only after the sauce is hot and off the fire or it may lump.*

*Serve with Sauvignon Blanc or Chardonnay.*

# PEACH SORBET

| | |
|---|---|
| 4 | peaches, fresh, pitted |
| 1/2 | cup orange marmalade |
| 1/2 | cup orange Muscat wine or other dessert wine |
| 1 | teaspoon lemon juice |
| | honey to taste (careful!) |
| | strawberries, fresh (or other fruit) |
| | lemon juice to taste |
| | mint leaves |

Simply blend first 5 ingredients in a food processor or through the fine sieve of a food mill and freeze overnight, stirring occasionally as it freezes. The next day, scrape out small balls using an ice cream scoop. Makes 12 sorbets or 6 desserts.

Serve on a little fresh strawberry sauce made by blending a few strawberries, lemon juice and honey. Garnish with mint.

*We serve a refreshing fruit ice before the entree after the appetizer, soup, and salad to give the taste buds a breather.*

## LAST CHANCE SALOON

The Last Chance Saloon is located below the Navigator Restaurant in Keystone Village. Originally opened in 1979 as "The Silver Slipper", the last few years Village patrons have realized our saloon *is* their "last chance". . .serving hearty pizza, subs and refreshing drinks from our fully stocked bar between 4:00 p.m. and 12:00 midnight. To add to the fun, the "Chance" offers live entertainment almost year-round—games during the summer, apres ski entertainment during the ski season and private-party capabilities. The fresh-dough pizza, with a choice of 13 delicious toppings, is still the main attraction: 3 sizes ranging from personal to group, plus Sicilian style; and a combination special that can't be beat. "To-Go" orders are also accepted. Join the Chance crowd for cold libations, good food, and lots of fun.

# THE TELEMARK

3/4    ounce Grand Marnier
3/4    ounce White Creme de Menthe
     coffee
     hot chocolate
     whipped cream
     cherry for garnish

Pour liqueurs into large mug. Add coffee and hot chocolate in equal portions. Stir together and top with whipped cream. Garnish with cherry . or . . . remove feet from ski boots and pour over tops of toes. . call your doctor. If pain persists. Your probably have frostbite!

# MUSKADONOVICH

1    cup ice
1/2    shot Cognac
1/2    shot Triple Sec
     lemon wedge
     sugar

In a shaker glass combine one cup ice, one-half shot Cognac and one-half shot Triple Sec. Shake briskly and pour into shot glass. Coat lemon wedge with sugar. Yell "MUSKADONO-VICH", then drink shot and bite into lemon wedge.

# COMBINATION SPECIAL

     white dough
     pizza sauce
     black olives, sliced
     pepperoni, sliced
     Italian sausage, sauteed
     mushrooms, sliced
     onions, diced
     mozzarella cheese, shredded

Place pizza dough onto round, 10-inch pan. Add amount of sauce desired (3 to 4 ounces). Place remaining ingredients over sauce, cheese last. Bake in a 500 degree oven for 12 to 15 minutes or until cheese browns. Slice into 8 pieces and serve. Serves 2 to 3 persons (or one large person).

# THE NAVIGATOR

## THE NAVIGATOR

The Navigator Restaurant has been serving great seafood and steaks since 1978. Situated on the edge of scenic Keystone Lake, owner Alfonso "Poncho" Guerrero's vision of having great seafood in the mountains has become a reality including Rocky Mountain Trout, New Zealand Grouper, Cajun Blackened Mahi-Mahi, broiled Norwegian Salmon, and live Maine Lobster. There are great beef and poultry dishes as well. With every entree you receive unlimited trips to our salad bar, featuring our legendary clam chowder. Our oyster bar is open daily from 4:30 to 6:00 p.m. and the dining room begins serving at 6:00 p.m. during summer and 5:30 p.m. during winter. The Navigator—by the lake in the heart of Keystone Village—has gained the attention of Colorado travelers, as well as the locals, for being one of the finest seafood restaurants in the Rockies.

## SHRIMP IN THE SHELL

| | |
|---|---|
| 1/2 | gallon water |
| | small bunch of parsley |
| 1/4 | whole lemon |
| 2 | stalks celery |
| 1/4 | whole onion |
| 1/2 | ounce black peppercorns |
| 2 | whole cloves |
| 1 | pound shrimp in their shell (21 to 25 per pound, thawed) |

Combine all ingredients except shrimp in cooking pot and bring to a low boil for 30 minutes. Add shrimp to boiling water and cook until boiling resumes again. (You can test readiness by cutting shrimp in two—the meat should be all white with no hint of translucence.)

Remove and cool quickly under cold running water. After cooling, store in refrigerator and serve with cocktail sauce and lemon wedges.

*The shrimp may be peeled and deveined if desired.*

## SKILLET OF MUSHROOMS

| | |
|---|---|
| 1 | cup medium-diced onions |
| 1/4 | cup butter |
| 1 | teaspoon garlic puree |
| 1 | teaspoon onion powder |
| 1 | ounce beef base |
| 1/2 | teaspoon white pepper |
| 1 | pound fresh, medium, whole mushrooms |
| 2 | ounces Sauterne |
| 1 | ounce cooking sherry |
| 1/3 | cup water |
| 1/4 | cup chopped scallions |
| 2 | tablespoons diced red pepper |

In medium saucepan or skillet, saute onions in butter until transparent. Add spices and seasonings and saute 2 or 3 more minutes. Add mushrooms, Sauterne, sherry and water. Let cook until most of mushrooms are covered in their own juices. Just before serving add freshly-chopped scallions and diced red pepper for extra color. Serves 6 to 8.

*Excellent when served with fresh baked bread and your favorite glass of wine.*

松林莊

# PINEWOOD VILLAGE

## PINEWOOD VILLAGE CHINESE RESTAURANT

In the Argentine Plaza, only a few steps down from Keystone Village you will find Pinewood Village, a unique Chinese restaurant serving Szechuan and Mandarin style cuisine. At your table overlooking the Snake River you will enjoy your favorite dishes, not only superbly prepared but beautifully presented. Specialties of the house include the following creations of a "Seafood Combination" containing shrimp, scallops and lobster and "Boneless Roast Duck with Triple Mushrooms", delicately prepared and deep fried to a gold brown. The chef in residence has 20 years of experience prior to the Pinewood Village in both Hong Kong and New York City. He will be happy to serve you beginning at 11:00 a.m. on weekdays and 12:00 noon on Saturday and Sunday.

# BONELESS ROAST DUCK

| 1 | 6 pound duck |
| 2 | teaspoons salt |
| 2 | green onions, chopped |
| 1 | garlic clove, crushed with knife |
| 1/4 | cup white wine |
| 1 | inch ginger root |
| | soy bean oil |
| 1/8 | teaspoon garlic powder |
| 1/8 | teaspoon ground ginger |
| 1 | teaspoon soy sauce |
| 1/8 | teaspoon sugar |
| 1 | teaspoon oyster flavored sauce* |
| 8 | ounces vegetables (Chinese cabbage, broccoli, black mushrooms*, summer oyster mushrooms*, straw mushrooms*, bamboo shoots, water chestnuts) |
| 1 | teaspoon sesame oil |
| 1-2 | teaspoons cornstarch dissolved in water |

*Duck:* Place duck in large container. Combine next 5 ingredients into a marinade and pour over duck. Cover and marinate in refrigerator over night. Cut duck in half and remove all bones. Deep fry 3 to 4 minutes in soy bean oil. Drain, slice and place on platter.

*Sauce:* Cook garlic powder, ginger, soy sauce, sugar, oyster sauce and vegetables in oil in hot wok or heavy pan. Add cornstarch to thicken. Can add water if needed for thinner consistency. Pour over duck and serve.

# SEAFOOD COMBINATION

| 4-5 | large shrimp |
| 6 | large sea scallops |
| 3 | ounces lobster meat |
| 8 | ounces vegetables (Chinese cabbage, broccoli, black mushrooms*, summer oyster mushrooms*, straw mushrooms*, bamboo shoots, water chestnuts) |
| 1 | teaspoon white wine |
| 1-1/2 | cups chicken stock |
| 1/3 | teaspoon salt |
| 1/3 | teaspoon sugar |
| | pinch monosodium glutamate (MSG) |
| 1/3 | teaspoon garlic powder |
| 1 | teaspoon sesame oil |
| 1-2 | teaspoons cornstarch dissolved in water |

Put seafood and vegetables into boiling water to cover, add wine and bring to second boil. Remove from heat and drain. Place back on high heat, add chicken stock, salt, sugar, MSG, garlic powder and oil. When hot, add dissolved cornstarch and stir until thick. Serve on hot platter with rice.

*Can be found in Oriental food store.

## SKI TIP LODGE

Formerly a stagecoach stop in the 1800s, this cozy lodge has been turned into Summit County's favorite country inn. Originally owned by Max and Edna Dercum and purchased in 1984 by Keystone Resort, Ski Tip retains the comfortable image and warmth reminiscent of days gone by. The architecture of the Lodge is of large logs, beams and huge fireplaces, and is a wonderful choice for families, couples or single persons. Breakfasts and dinners are included at Ski Tip with lodging. Dinner is served between 6:00 and 9:30 p.m. and Sunday Brunch is served from 9:00 a.m. to 1:00 p.m. Reservations for dinner and Sunday Brunch are suggested.

# CHICKEN SKI TIP

| 1 | tablespoon butter |
|---|---|
| 1 | small onion, diced |
| 8 | ounces breakfast sausage, bulk |
| 1 | pound fresh spinach, cleaned, chopped |
| 1/2 | cup flour |
| 1 | cup milk |
| 5 | double breasts of chicken (6 ounces each), skinned, boned and cartilage removed |
| 4 | cups flour |
| 1-1/2 | pounds butter or margarine, softened |
| 1-1/2 | cups sour cream |
| 3 | whole eggs |
| 1 | egg yolk |
| 1/4 | cup water or milk |

Melt butter in saute pan, add onion and sausage. Cook until sausage is cooked through. Drain most of residual fat. Add spinach and stir in until spinach is wilted. Add 1/2 cup flour and stir until blended. Add 1 cup milk and stir until mixture is thickened. Transfer into a bowl and refrigerate.

Pound chicken until uniform in thickness. Tear off a piece of plastic wrap 18-inches long and place on a board. Arrange chicken breasts side by side along the center of the wrap. Take the sausage and spinach mixture and form into a cylinder shape and lie it along the center of the chicken breasts. Take one of the long sides of the wrap and roll the chicken around the stuffing so that the chicken covers all of the stuffing. Twist the ends of the wrap to hold the chicken together and place on a sheet pan and refrigerate. The chicken can be frozen at this point and thawed for later use.

Place flour in medium-sized bowl; cut in butter or margarine. Add 1-1/2 cups sour cream and blend in eggs. Flour a board; roll out into a large rectangle. Unroll chicken from plastic wrap onto the dough on one side of the rectangle. Fold or roll the other half of the dough over the chicken and cut off excess dough. Crimp the edges all around the chicken with a fork. Place on a greased sheet pan. Brush with a beaten mixture of egg yolk and water. Bake in a preheated 350 degree oven for 45 minutes or until light golden brown.

*Serve with a supreme sauce or white sauce if desired and a bottle of Chardonnay wine.*

# DRIEMEYER STEAK ROQUEFORT

| | |
|---|---|
| 1 | tablespoon butter |
| 1 | tablespoon flour |
| 1/4 | cup dry white wine |
| 3/4 | cup cream |
| 1/2 | cup Roquefort cheese |
| | salt |
| | pepper, freshly ground |
| | pinch of cayenne |
| 2-4 | well-marbled steaks of your choice (We recommend T-bone, seasoned to your liking.) |

*Sauce:* Melt butter in saucepan. Add flour and stir with a whip until thoroughly blended and bubbling. Do not brown. Add wine and continue to stir while boiling for 2 minutes. Add cream slowly, stirring. Bring to a simmer and cook for 20 minutes or until mixture coats a spoon. Add cheese and seasonings, barely returning to boil and remove from heat.

Broil or grill steaks to your preference. Top each steak with a generous portion of the Roquefort sauce.

*The cheese proportion and seasonings may be adjusted to personal taste. Two to four tablespoons of beef stock may be added at the same time as the cream. Increase the cooking time for this addition.*

*Serve with a rich, full-bodied Cabernet Sauvignon or Merlot wine.*

# THE RESTAURANTS OF KEYSTONE MOUNTAIN

When you decide to take a break from a day of skiing or hiking you will find a wide range of atmospheres awaiting you at Keystone Mountain, from fresh shrimp and oyster bars, and outdoor barbeques to a full-service sit-down restaurant.

Fresh shrimp and oyster bars have been introduced along with outdoor barbeques featuring authentic mesquite-smoked ribs and chicken and hearty barbeque beef sandwiches with corn on the cob, baked beans, cold beer and wine coolers.

At the base of Keystone Mountain you will find the **Pavilion Café** (sometimes known as **Gassy's**), our sit-down, full-service restaurant designed to provide you with a refreshing alternative to cafeteria fast food. Featured among other items are fresh homemade soups, hearty prime rib sandwiches, chicken enchiladas, fresh baked breads and a hot fudge brownie sundae for dessert. For dinner, the Pavilion Café provides relaxing family dining at reasonable prices.

Keystone is the only place in Summit County you can take a gondola ride to an elevation of 11,640 feet to the Summit House and find **Der Fondue Chessel**, a unique experience in the Swiss tradition serving a variety of fondues in an atmosphere of candles and checkered tablecloths. Enjoy the view of Keystone Mountain at night in front of the fireplace while listening to live entertainment with the feel of the mountains.

Also while at the mountain top, you can enjoy the hearty, homemade soups, sandwiches, fresh shrimp and pasta salads at **Soup's On** at the Summit House or stop at the indoor/outdoor **Barbeque at the Summit** serving smoked ribs and chicken, barbeque beef sandwiches, German sausage with sauerkraut and red hot Texas-style chili.

While enjoying either the blazing fireplace or any one of the sun drenched decks you will experience that unmatched "Colorado Mountain High"!

## PAVILION CAFE/GASSY'S — SEAFOOD CHOWDER

| | |
|---|---|
| 3 | tablespoons butter |
| 1 | medium diced onion |
| 2 | stalks diced celery |
| 1 | medium diced sweet red pepper |
| 1/4 | teaspoon thyme |
| 1 | bay leaf |
| 1 | clove minced garlic |
| 1 | cup white wine |
| 5 | tablespoons flour |
| 6 | cups fish broth or clam juice |
| 1 | cup baby shrimp* |
| 1 | cup scallops* |
| 1 | cup clams* |
| 1 | cup sliced mushrooms |
| 1 | cup shredded mild or medium Cheddar cheese |
| 1/2 | cup cream or half and half |

In 2-quart pot, melt butter, add onion, celery, pepper, thyme, bay leaf and garlic. Saute over medium heat for 5 minutes. Add white wine and continue cooking until volume is reduced by half. Add flour and mix well, cooking an additional 2 to 3 minutes. Slowly add fish broth or clam juice or combination of the two. While stirring constantly, add seafood and mushrooms, simmer over low heat about 15 minutes. Reduce heat to low and stir in cheese. Add salt to taste. Add cream before serving. Serve with fresh hard rolls.

———————

*Other seafoods may be used.

# Der FONDUE CHESSEL

At Keystone Mountain's Summit House. Serving nightly from 4:00-9:00 P.M. For apres-ski or during night skiing.

## DER FONDUE CHESSEL — CHOCOLATE FONDUE

| | |
|---|---|
| 8 | ounces grated and weighed Ghiradelli chocolate |
| 2 | ounces Triple Sec |
| 6 | ounces heavy whipping cream |

strawberries halved
pineapple cut bite-sized
banana cut bite-sized
orange wedges
pound cake in 1-inch cubes
cantaloupe cut bite-sized
apple wedges

Melt chocolate gradually in top of double boiler. Add Triple Sec and heavy whipping cream and transfer to fondue pot. Dip fruit and cake in fondue.

## SOUP'S ON — POTATO SALAD

| | |
|---|---|
| 5 | cups coarsely-diced potatoes |
| 1/8 | teaspoon cayenne pepper |
| 3/4 | cup mayonnaise |
| 1 | tablespoon prepared mustard |
| | salt to taste |
| 4 | tablespoons sweet pickle relish |
| 1/2 | cup finely-diced celery |
| 2 | eggs, peeled and chopped |

Boil potatoes in water with cayenne pepper. Drain very well. Combine mayonnaise, mustard, salt and sweet relish. Add with celery and eggs to potatoes, mixing together by hand. Adjust seasoning to taste. Serves 4.

# BARBEQUE AT THE SUMMIT — TEXAS STYLE CHILI

**BARBEQUE**
AT THE SUMMIT

| | |
|---|---|
| 4 | strips bacon, chopped |
| 1 | pound beef, in 1-inch cubes |
| 1 | pound pork, in 1-inch cubes |
| 1/2 | pound chorizo (Mexican-style sausage) |
| 1 | medium onion, diced |
| 2 | medium green peppers, diced |
| 1 | cup green chilies, chopped |
| 2 | Jalapenos, chopped (canned or pickled) |
| 2 | tablespoons chili powder |
| 1 | teaspoon minced garlic |
| 1/4 | teaspoon cayenne pepper (or to taste) |
| 1/2 | teaspoon oregano |
| 1 | cup diced tomatoes |
| 12 | ounces beer |
| 3 | cups water |

Place bacon in heavy bottomed saucepan and saute over medium heat until it begins to brown. Add beef, pork and chorizo and brown well. Lower heat; add onions, green peppers, green chilies, Jalapenos, chili powder, garlic, cayenne pepper and oregano. Cook an additional 5 minutes; add tomatoes, beer and water. Stir well. Cover and simmer over low heat approximately 1-1/2 hours or until beef is very tender. Serve with cold beer and Texas toast. Serves 6.

*For hotter chili add more Jalapenos.*

# INDEX

Hospitality is evident in the award-winning Keystone Lodge.

## APPETIZERS

Artichoke-Ham Bites ............................ 12
Carol's "Knock-'Em Dead" Artichokes ............. 12
Chafing Dish Chili Sausage Appetizer ............ 13
Chicken Wings Oriental ......................... 11
Crab Meat Loaf ................................ 14
Fresh Mussels with Pasta ...................... 169
Great Guacamole ................................ 6
Guacamole Dip .................................. 6
Hawaiian Bread Appetizer ....................... 9
Herring ....................................... 13
Hot Crab 'n' Cheese Dip ....................... 14
Layered Taco Dip ............................... 5
Little Pizzas ................................. 10
Mexican Appetizer .............................. 7
Mom's Meatballs ............................... 16
Monterey Cheese Bake ........................... 5
Montezuma Spinach Dip .......................... 8
Paul's Stuffed Bread .......................... 10
Quicksilver Cheeseball ......................... 4
Rumaki ........................................ 15
Salami Pinwheels .............................. 15
Shrimp in the Shell .......................... 174
Skillet of Mushrooms ......................... 174
Snack Crackers ................................ 11
Sourdough Goldmine ............................. 9
Spinach Balls .................................. 4
Stuffed Mushrooms .............................. 7
Triple Cheese Appetizer Wheel .................. 3
Vegetable Dip .................................. 8

## SOUPS AND STEWS

Alfie Packer Stew ............................. 31
Bean Soup with Apples ......................... 26
Beef Ragout ................................... 34
Cheery Chowder ................................ 30
Chicken-Cheese Soup ........................... 19
Chili ......................................... 34
Chili Dog Stew ................................ 31
Christmas Eve Potage .......................... 24
Creamed Artichoke Soup ........................ 25
Dutch Onion Soup .............................. 21
Easy Bookbinder's Seafood Bisque .............. 27
Easy Stew ..................................... 32
Fish Soup from the Cupboard ................... 20
Flemish Stew .................................. 32
French Onion Soup ............................ 161
Garden Soup ................................... 24
Grandma's Homemade Tomato Soup ................ 25
Italian Endive Soup ........................... 21
Jersey Lilly Chili ............................ 36
Jim Tulley's Stew ............................. 33
Macho Chili ................................... 35
Mexican Cheese Soup ........................... 20
Old Fashioned Beef Stew ...................... 154

188

Oregon Bean Soup . . . . . . . . . . . . . . . . . . . . . . . 26
Potato Vegetable Soup . . . . . . . . . . . . . . . . . . . . . 23
Pumpkin Bisque . . . . . . . . . . . . . . . . . . . . . . . . . 28
Quick and Easy Broccoli Soup . . . . . . . . . . . . . . 22
Seafood Chowder . . . . . . . . . . . . . . . . . . . . . . . . 181
Shrimp Bisque . . . . . . . . . . . . . . . . . . . . . . . . . . 29
Ski-Slope Stew . . . . . . . . . . . . . . . . . . . . . . . . . . 33
Swedish Pea Soup . . . . . . . . . . . . . . . . . . . . . . . 22
Take Your Choice Chowder . . . . . . . . . . . . . . . . 29
Texas Style Chili . . . . . . . . . . . . . . . . . . . . . . . . 184
World's Greatest Vegetable Soup . . . . . . . . . . . . 27

## BREADS

Alpentop Whole Wheat Bread . . . . . . . . . . . . . . 152
Apple Walnut Bread . . . . . . . . . . . . . . . . . . . . . . 39
Banana Nut Bread . . . . . . . . . . . . . . . . . . . . . . . 39
Bran Muffins Plus . . . . . . . . . . . . . . . . . . . . . . . 45
Butter Brickle Bread . . . . . . . . . . . . . . . . . . . . . 40
Buttermilk Rolls . . . . . . . . . . . . . . . . . . . . . . . . 44
Corn Bread—Sugarless! . . . . . . . . . . . . . . . . . . . 41
Dill Bread . . . . . . . . . . . . . . . . . . . . . . . . . . . . . 41
Healthy Bran Muffins . . . . . . . . . . . . . . . . . . . . 45
Herb Bread . . . . . . . . . . . . . . . . . . . . . . . . . . . . 47
Mighty Muffins . . . . . . . . . . . . . . . . . . . . . . . . . 46
Pita Bread . . . . . . . . . . . . . . . . . . . . . . . . . . . . . 47
Rhubarb Bread . . . . . . . . . . . . . . . . . . . . . . . . . 40
Rum Batter French Toast . . . . . . . . . . . . . . . . . 161
Rye Bread . . . . . . . . . . . . . . . . . . . . . . . . . . . . . 42

Texas Toast . . . . . . . . . . . . . . . . . . . . . . . . . . . . 46
Three-Grain Bread . . . . . . . . . . . . . . . . . . . . . . 43
Whole Wheat Bread . . . . . . . . . . . . . . . . . . . . . 44

## ENTREES

Ala Armond—A Crustless Quiche . . . . . . . . . . . . 52
Apple Chicken . . . . . . . . . . . . . . . . . . . . . . . . . . 58
Aunt Shirley's Barbeque Sauce . . . . . . . . . . . . . 86
Barbeque for a Crowd . . . . . . . . . . . . . . . . . . . . 62
Barbeque Sauce . . . . . . . . . . . . . . . . . . . . . . . . . 86
Barbequed Short Ribs . . . . . . . . . . . . . . . . . . . . 63
Bastard Barbeque Chicken . . . . . . . . . . . . . . . . 59
Beef and Wild Rice Casserole . . . . . . . . . . . . . . 72
Beef Napoleon . . . . . . . . . . . . . . . . . . . . . . . . . . 61
Boneless Roast Duck . . . . . . . . . . . . . . . . . . . . . 176
Bratwurst with Cheese and Sauerkraut . . . . . . . 166
Broiled Fish with Artichoke-Caper Sauce . . . . . . 83
Broiled Scallops with Garlic and Cheese Bread
    Crumbs . . . . . . . . . . . . . . . . . . . . . . . . . . . . . 159
Brownie's Burgers . . . . . . . . . . . . . . . . . . . . . . . 64
Cabbage Rolls . . . . . . . . . . . . . . . . . . . . . . . . . . 67
Cheese Enchiladas . . . . . . . . . . . . . . . . . . . . . . . 81
Chicken and Rice Casserole . . . . . . . . . . . . . . . . 54
Chicken-Artichoke Casserole . . . . . . . . . . . . . . . 55
Chicken Crepes . . . . . . . . . . . . . . . . . . . . . . . . . 51
Chicken Divan . . . . . . . . . . . . . . . . . . . . . . . . . . 53
Chicken Ibo . . . . . . . . . . . . . . . . . . . . . . . . . . . . 56
Chicken Paradise . . . . . . . . . . . . . . . . . . . . . . . . 57

Chicken Rolls . . . . . . . . . . . . . . . . . . . . . . . . . . . . . . 54
Chicken Ski Tip . . . . . . . . . . . . . . . . . . . . . . . . . . . . 178
Colorado Broiled Trout . . . . . . . . . . . . . . . . . . . . . . . 82
Combination Special . . . . . . . . . . . . . . . . . . . . . . . . 172
Crepe-a-Dilla . . . . . . . . . . . . . . . . . . . . . . . . . . . . . 165
Crusty Beef, Cheese and Noodle Casserole . . . . . . . . . . . 72
Curried Chicken and Rice . . . . . . . . . . . . . . . . . . . . . 53
Dad Shive's Favorite Boiled Dinner . . . . . . . . . . . . . . . 75
Day-Before Mazzetti Casserole . . . . . . . . . . . . . . . . . . 73
Driemeyer Steak Roquefort . . . . . . . . . . . . . . . . . . . 179
Easy Lasagna . . . . . . . . . . . . . . . . . . . . . . . . . . . . . 71
Easy One-Step Lasagna . . . . . . . . . . . . . . . . . . . . . . . 69
El Dorado Casserole . . . . . . . . . . . . . . . . . . . . . . . . . 69
Fajitas . . . . . . . . . . . . . . . . . . . . . . . . . . . . . . . . . . 67
Filet Mignon . . . . . . . . . . . . . . . . . . . . . . . . . . . . . 159
Flank Steak Marinade . . . . . . . . . . . . . . . . . . . . . . . . 63
Fried Rainbow Trout . . . . . . . . . . . . . . . . . . . . . . . . 84
Grilled Breast of Wild Duck . . . . . . . . . . . . . . . . . . . 85
Honey-Fried Fish . . . . . . . . . . . . . . . . . . . . . . . . . . . 84
Italian Beef . . . . . . . . . . . . . . . . . . . . . . . . . . . . . . 66
King Ranch Kitchen Casserole . . . . . . . . . . . . . . . . . . 57
Lamb Shanks . . . . . . . . . . . . . . . . . . . . . . . . . . . . . 77
Lasagna . . . . . . . . . . . . . . . . . . . . . . . . . . . . . . . . . 70
Made Rites . . . . . . . . . . . . . . . . . . . . . . . . . . . . . . 64
Mrs. Kmet's Chicken . . . . . . . . . . . . . . . . . . . . . . . . 55
Mushroom Wine Sauce . . . . . . . . . . . . . . . . . . . . . . . 87
Mustard Chicken . . . . . . . . . . . . . . . . . . . . . . . . . . . 52

Oriental Beef Steak Strips . . . . . . . . . . . . . . . . . . . . . 66
Peru Creek Omelet for Two . . . . . . . . . . . . . . . . . . . . 80
Pork Chop Casserole . . . . . . . . . . . . . . . . . . . . . . . . 74
Pork Roast with Lemon or "Porc au Citron" . . . . . . . . . 73
Prime Rib . . . . . . . . . . . . . . . . . . . . . . . . . . . . . . . 60
Provinicial Torte . . . . . . . . . . . . . . . . . . . . . . . . . . 152
Puffy Fondue . . . . . . . . . . . . . . . . . . . . . . . . . . . . . 79
Sauce for Wild Fowl . . . . . . . . . . . . . . . . . . . . . . . . 88
Sausage Brunch . . . . . . . . . . . . . . . . . . . . . . . . . . . 76
Sausage Stroganoff . . . . . . . . . . . . . . . . . . . . . . . . . 76
Savory Sauce for Lamb . . . . . . . . . . . . . . . . . . . . . . . 87
Seafood Combination . . . . . . . . . . . . . . . . . . . . . . . 176
Shrimp Dijon . . . . . . . . . . . . . . . . . . . . . . . . . . . . 164
Sour Cream Mix Enchiladas Casserole . . . . . . . . . . . . . 60
Spaghetti Pie . . . . . . . . . . . . . . . . . . . . . . . . . . . . . 68
Spinach and Ham Strata . . . . . . . . . . . . . . . . . . . . . . 74
Steak Baste . . . . . . . . . . . . . . . . . . . . . . . . . . . . . . 88
Sunny's Chinese Dish . . . . . . . . . . . . . . . . . . . . . . . . 65
Super Chicken . . . . . . . . . . . . . . . . . . . . . . . . . . . . 58
Super Simple Chicken Breasts with Chipped Beef . . . . . . 59
Swiss Cheese Pie . . . . . . . . . . . . . . . . . . . . . . . . . . . 78
Teriyaki Chicken . . . . . . . . . . . . . . . . . . . . . . . . . . 157
Texas Quiche . . . . . . . . . . . . . . . . . . . . . . . . . . . . . 79
Veal with Pistachio and Tomato Basil Sauce . . . . . . . . . 163
Walleye and Bacon Sandwiches, Minnesota Style . . . . . . 82
Western Barbeque Brisket . . . . . . . . . . . . . . . . . . . . . 62

## VEGETABLES AND SIDE DISHES

Asparagus Casserole ............................... 91
Broccoli-Rice Casserole .......................... 93
Brown Rice ....................................... 98
Celery Wedges Parmesan ........................... 94
Cheezy Vegetable Casserole ...................... 101
Coleman Corn Pudding ............................. 95
Escalloped Corn .................................. 94
Green Bean Casserole ............................. 91
Hash Browns ...................................... 96
Heavenly Onions .................................. 95
Kapusta (Sweet Polish Sauerkraut) ................ 99
Oven Rice ........................................ 98
Pat's Potatoes ................................... 97
Potatoes Romanoff ................................ 97
Puree of Parsnips ................................ 96
Russian Vegetable Pie ........................... 102
Savory Baked Garbanzo Beans ...................... 92
Southern Zucchini Casserole ..................... 101
Spinach/Noodle Casserole ........................ 100
Tomato Pie ...................................... 100
Upper Mill Terrace Broccoli Casserole ............ 93
Wild Rice ........................................ 99

## SALADS AND SALAD DRESSINGS

Aunt Pauline's Salad ............................ 105
B.L.T. Salad .................................... 108
Blueberry-Cream Gelatin Salad ................... 113

Broccoli Salad .................................. 105
Carol Brown's Herb Dressing ..................... 114
Cauliflower Salad ............................... 107
Chicken Liver Salad ............................. 110
Chili Taco Salad ................................ 110
Cranberry Compote ............................... 111
Cranberry Salad ................................. 111
Curried Tomato Salad ............................ 107
Easy Salad ...................................... 114
Five-Layer Salad ................................ 108
Fix 'n' Ski Salad ............................... 112
Fresh Tarragon Spinach Salad .................... 106
Joe's World Famous Tabouli ...................... 109
Layer Salad ..................................... 106
Mad River Valley French Dressing ................ 115
Oak Park Potato Salad ........................... 109
Peaches and Cream Gelatin Salad ................. 113
Poppy Seed Dressing ............................. 156
Potato Salad .................................... 183
Tangy Cran-Raspberry Holiday Mold ............... 112

## DESSERTS

Baked Caramel Corn .............................. 142
Baked Indian Pudding ............................ 136
Beer Nuts (Maple Sugar Coated Peanuts) .......... 140
Chocolate au Provence ........................... 135
Chocolate Bon Bons .............................. 139
Chocolate Eclair Cake ........................... 126

Chocolate Fondue . . . . . . . . . . . . . . . . . . . . . . . . . . . . 182
Chocolate Mint Brownies . . . . . . . . . . . . . . . . . . . . . 120
Chocolate Pear Tart . . . . . . . . . . . . . . . . . . . . . . . . . 153
Chocolate Sauce . . . . . . . . . . . . . . . . . . . . . . . . . . . . 137
Christmas Cranberry Dessert . . . . . . . . . . . . . . . . . . 121
Cookies and Cream Dessert . . . . . . . . . . . . . . . . . . . 133
Cream Candy . . . . . . . . . . . . . . . . . . . . . . . . . . . . . . 139
Cream Puffs . . . . . . . . . . . . . . . . . . . . . . . . . . . . . . . 122
Crowned Carrot Cake . . . . . . . . . . . . . . . . . . . . . . . 128
Danish Cheesecake . . . . . . . . . . . . . . . . . . . . . . . . . 121
Easy Old Fashioned Sugar Cookies . . . . . . . . . . . . . 132
Elegant Orange Cake . . . . . . . . . . . . . . . . . . . . . . . . 127
Famous Hot Fudge Sauce . . . . . . . . . . . . . . . . . . . . 137
Fine Oatmeal Cookies . . . . . . . . . . . . . . . . . . . . . . . 131
French Chocolate Truffles . . . . . . . . . . . . . . . . . . . 141
Gingerbread Sauce . . . . . . . . . . . . . . . . . . . . . . . . . 138
Grandma Laschanzky's Bulls Eyes (Swedish Pastry) . . . . 130
Grandma Perkins's Old Fashioned Sugar Cookies . . . . . . 131
Grandma's Vanilla Ice Cream . . . . . . . . . . . . . . . . . 136
Jane Bergman's Christmas Bundt . . . . . . . . . . . . . . . 129
Kahlua-Banana Crepe . . . . . . . . . . . . . . . . . . . . . . . 167
Lemon Bars . . . . . . . . . . . . . . . . . . . . . . . . . . . . . . . 133
Lois's Chocolate Cake . . . . . . . . . . . . . . . . . . . . . . . 126
Marshmallow Fudgies . . . . . . . . . . . . . . . . . . . . . . . 134
Mountain Delight's Chocolate Pizza . . . . . . . . . . . . 142
Mudd Pie . . . . . . . . . . . . . . . . . . . . . . . . . . . . . . . . 156
Never Fail Candy . . . . . . . . . . . . . . . . . . . . . . . . . . 138

Open Faced Apple Pie . . . . . . . . . . . . . . . . . . . . . . . 124
Peach Sorbet . . . . . . . . . . . . . . . . . . . . . . . . . . . . . . 170
Peanut Brittle . . . . . . . . . . . . . . . . . . . . . . . . . . . . . 140
Pear Pie . . . . . . . . . . . . . . . . . . . . . . . . . . . . . . . . . . 125
Pecan Pie . . . . . . . . . . . . . . . . . . . . . . . . . . . . . . . . 124
Pecan Torte . . . . . . . . . . . . . . . . . . . . . . . . . . . . . . 123
Popular Cup Cakes . . . . . . . . . . . . . . . . . . . . . . . . . 129
Quick Molasses Sugar Cookies . . . . . . . . . . . . . . . . 132
Salted Nut Bars . . . . . . . . . . . . . . . . . . . . . . . . . . . 141
Shredded Newspaper Cake . . . . . . . . . . . . . . . . . . . 119

## BEVERAGES

Homemade Bailey's Irish Cream . . . . . . . . . . . . . . . 146
Hot Cider . . . . . . . . . . . . . . . . . . . . . . . . . . . . . . . . 148
Hot Cranberry Punch . . . . . . . . . . . . . . . . . . . . . . . 148
Ice Float . . . . . . . . . . . . . . . . . . . . . . . . . . . . . . . . . 147
Kahlua . . . . . . . . . . . . . . . . . . . . . . . . . . . . . . . . . . 146
Muskadonovich . . . . . . . . . . . . . . . . . . . . . . . . . . . 172
Pilgrim's Progress . . . . . . . . . . . . . . . . . . . . . . . . . . 147
Spring Flings . . . . . . . . . . . . . . . . . . . . . . . . . . . . . 145
The Telemark . . . . . . . . . . . . . . . . . . . . . . . . . . . . . 172
Wassail . . . . . . . . . . . . . . . . . . . . . . . . . . . . . . . . . . 145

Notes

Notes

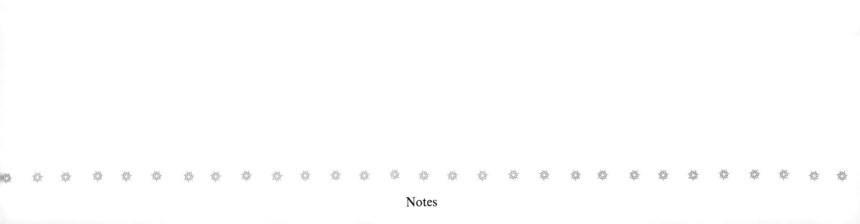

Notes

Notes

Carolyn (Kay) R. Shive, Publisher
Lake Macbride
Solon, Iowa  52333

Please send me _____ copies of *The Keystone Cookbook—A Mountain of Delights* at $14.95 each plus $1.50 postage and handling per book. Check or money order will be made payable to "Keystone Cookbook". Thank you.

Name _____

Street _____

City _____ State _____ Zip _____

---

## THE KEYSTONE COOKBOOK—A MOUNTAIN OF DELIGHTS

Carolyn (Kay) R. Shive, Publisher
Lake Macbride
Solon, Iowa  52333

Please send me _____ copies of *The Keystone Cookbook—A Mountain of Delights* at $14.95 each plus $1.50 postage and handling per book. Check or money order will be made payable to "Keystone Cookbook". Thank you.

Name _____

Street _____

City _____ State _____ Zip _____